THE EVERYTHING®
Cooking for Dogs Book

Dear Reader,

Who would have ever thought that owning two dogs, one picky eater and one with allergies, would change my life? Well, combine that with the love of baking and an entrepreneurial spirit, and you get robbie dawg, inc. Located in Brooklyn, New York, robbie dawg's goal has always been to provide pet owners with the quality of product that they would bake themselves if they had the time.

Time is ever so precious, and the demands of work and family leave little or no time for extras. The exceptions to the rule seem to center on holidays, birthdays, or anniversaries, and the celebrations always revolve around food.

Modern dogs have been elevated to full-fledged members of the family. It seems fitting that they should also have a cookbook that encompasses all types of canine culinary delights. This cookbook offers recipes for healthy and flavorful biscuits, biscotti, birthday and celebration cakes, meals, and training treats. It also offers some basic nutritional guidelines, information on foods your dog should avoid, and tips for baking and cooking.

Thank you for allowing me to share my recipes. I hope you involve your family and build traditions for the members who are always happy to see you, who provide unconditional love, and who appreciate every kindness with the wag of a tail and a very wet kiss.

Lisa Fortunato
AKA Robbie and LuLu's M

The **EVERYTHING** Series

Editorial

Innovation Director	Paula Munier
Editorial Director	Laura M. Daly
Acquisitions Editor	Brielle K. Matson
Associate Development Editor	Elizabeth Kassab
Production Editor	Casey Ebert

Production

Director of Manufacturing	Susan Beale
Production Project Manager	Michelle Roy Kelly
Prepress	Matt LeBlanc Erick DaCosta
Interior Layout	Heather Barrett Brewster Brownville Colleen Cunningham Jennifer Oliveira
Series Cover Artist	Barry Littmann

THE
EVERYTHING®

COOKING
FOR DOGS
BOOK

150 quick and healthy recipes your dog will love!

Lisa Fortunato
Owner of robbie dawg, inc.

Adams Media
Avon, Massachusetts

This cookbook is dedicated to my parents, Mary and
AJ Fortunato, who taught me the joy of baking for one's family.

*   *   *

An Everything® Series Book.
Everything® and everything.com® are registered
trademarks of F+W Publications, Inc.

Published by Adams Media, an F+W Publications Company
57 Littlefield Street, Avon, MA 02322 U.S.A.
www.adamsmedia.com

ISBN 10: 1-59869-431-6
ISBN 13: 978-1-59869-431-4

Printed in Canada.

J I H G F E D C B A

Library of Congress Cataloging-in-Publication Data
Fortunato, Lisa.
The everything cooking for dogs book : 150 quick and
healthy recipes your dog will love! / Lisa Fortunato.
p. cm. – (An everything series book)
Includes bibliographical references.
ISBN-13: 978-1-59869-431-4 (pbk. : alk. paper)
ISBN-10: 1-59869-431-6 (pbk. : alk. paper)
1. Dogs–Food–Recipes. I. Title.
SF427.4.F67 2007
636.7'085–dc22
2007018978

*This book is available at quantity discounts for bulk purchases.
For information, please call 1-800-289-0963.*

Contents

13 Let's Have a Party! 167

15 Flavor Enhancers 193

14 Celebration Cakes 179

Acknowledgments

I'd like to sincerely thank the many people who have helped me throughout the writing process. Brielle Matson, my editor, whose patience, guidance, and encouragement has made the cookbook a reality. Elizabeth Kassab, my developmental editor, who had her dog, Baxter, taste-test many of the recipes during the editing process. My husband, John, and my son, Adam, who remain forever as the behind-the-scenes support group; and to Robbie and LuLu, without whom there would be no robbie dawg, inc., or organic dog biscuit recipes.

My cousin Michael Padula is a constant reminder of how the love and support of family can lead to great things, and my dear friend Peter Collins listens and listens and keeps me on track. I am also fortunate to have a hardworking and dedicated staff and thank them as they are truly appreciated: Amy Cheng, Chun Yi Deng, Kristin Mims-Barrow, Sharon Nelson, and Arturo Ramirez.

Introduction

Like any good cookbook, this one is organized into sections. This particular book includes recipes for dog biscuits, biscotti, main meals, celebration cakes, and fancy party appetizers and hors d'oeuvres. There are guidelines on the basic nutritional needs of dogs and recommended equipment and ingredients for ease of preparation.

The recipes are straight-forward, easy to follow, and jam-packed with helpful hints and informative facts to guide you along the way. There is a huge endorsement for cooking with organic and natural ingredients. The news reminds you almost daily about the effects of eating processed foods, preservatives, and trans fats. Not only can these foods have an adverse effect on your waistline, they can be devastating to your health as well. These concerns are no less important for your dog, as her body is smaller and more sensitive. Poor diet and nutrition can lead to illnesses and health problems in dogs at a more acute and accelerated rate than in humans.

The spring 2007 recall of more than $30 million of tainted dog food is only a further sign that taking control of what you feed your dog should be of paramount concern. Awareness is key, and this cookbook offers simple and small changes in diet and lifestyle that can dramatically affect your pet's well-being. This cookbook offers recipes to fill the void and guide you to a healthier way of cooking and baking.

You will find recipes for biscuits that incorporate fruits, vegetables, meats, and cheeses. The combinations are often savory without the addition of salt, spices, and sugar, and the flavors appeal both to your dog's sense of taste and your desire to provide an alternative to store-bought treats. There are biscotti recipes prepared with the same baking methods as traditional biscotti, where the biscuits are baked twice. The result is a genuinely crispy, hard snack, with roots in Italian recipes revised appropriately to be dog friendly. The cake recipes are simple. The addition of vegetables and cooked meats will satisfy your need to offer your dog a cake, but without the sugar and empty calories he doesn't need. Party recipes include everything from chicken broth ice pops to liver pâté napoleons.

The main meal section includes favorites such as Chicken Cacciatore, Beef Stew, Baked Fish Florentine, and even a recipe for Green Eggs and Ham. There are pasta and rice dishes that can soothe an upset stomach and a whole section on simple "gravies" that can be used as kibble flavor enhancers. There is also a section on baking your own training treats that guarantee you will be able to teach an old dog new tricks.

The ingredients called for in most of the recipes are simple staple items, but the emphasis is on using fresh and organic products. You will not find a single recipe that calls for the addition of sugar or salt. This cookbook has been designed to be a useful resource as well as a treasure trove of creative recipes that cater to your dog's health and nutritional needs while allowing you to be creative and have fun. Health issues and allergies are two of the major concerns that dog owners deal with on a daily basis. Learning to identify your own dog's digestive sensitivities will allow you to prepare the right foods. Common food intolerances such as sensitivity to wheat, gluten, and lactose are discussed and appropriate ingredient replacements are profiled. Even if you know your dog should not eat chocolate, you may be surprised to find grapes, raisins, and even citrus oils on the list of no-nos.

In the end, the hope is that this cookbook will become a reference tool for you and your family. Your dog is a member of your family, and although she cannot participate in the preparation, she will certainly appreciate your efforts.

Chapter 1

Dog Nutrition

Only fifty years ago, most dogs ate table scraps. Twenty-five years ago, cereal companies starting producing commercially prepared pet food to sell in supermarkets and agricultural feed stores. Today, grocery stores dedicate an entire aisle to food made specifically for pets. There are dry premium foods, convenient semimoist packets, gourmet diets, and specialty foods for puppies, adult dogs, older dogs, and, of course, overweight dogs. Most commercially prepared dog foods are made from a fixed formula of ingredients that will provide your dog with a balanced diet. But there is another way to make sure your dog eats properly—fixing her meals and treats yourself.

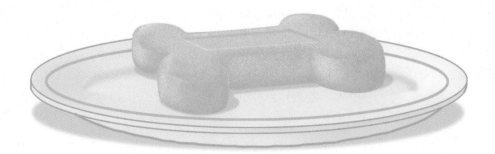

Dog Food Basics

Dog biscuits first appeared in England in the 1860s. The pet food industry in the United States began in earnest around the same time when breakfast cereal manufacturers began adding dried meat scraps to their dog meal to create a balanced canine diet. The canning of horsemeat as dog food began in the 1920s, and within ten years nearly 200 brands of canned food were available.

After World War II, dry foods gained popularity, and pet owners served canned meat over kibble. The pet food industry exploded with the production of canned and dry foods, and the development of convenient semimoist foods and snacks has created a $36 billion annual industry.

Kibble

Early kibble consisted of dough made from grains, flours, meat meals, dairy products, vitamins, and minerals baked in large pans. After baking, the dry slabs were broken into bite-size pieces. The development of the extrusion method, in which dough is pressed through a rotary machine that molds or shapes it into various pieces before baking, revolutionized the growing industry. Today, many kibbled foods are prepared in a mixing pressure cooker, and the resulting dough is extruded through a die and expanded with steam and air into small, porous nuggets. These nuggets are coated with a liquid fat, carbohydrate, or milk product for added calories and palatability.

Premium kibble consists of chicken, turkey, chicken meal, whole-grain brown rice flour, fruit, and vegetables. Vitamins, dried kelp, and ground flaxseed are healthy additions. Top-quality kibble is more expensive and is not available in most supermarkets, but it provides a strong basis for good and balanced nutrition. Organic kibble's popularity is increasing with the rest of the organic market. As public awareness grows, consumers will have more choices.

Semimoist Foods

Semimoist foods are cooked combinations of soybean meal, sugar, fresh meat or meat by-products, animal fat, preservatives, and humectants (wetting agents that allow the product to stay moist but not spoil). The dough is extruded into a variety of shapes to resemble chunks of meat to appeal to the pet owner. Coloring is added so the food resembles "red" meat. Try to avoid feeding your dog semimoist foods because they are high in salt and sugar.

 Essential

Elevated dog dishes are more comfortable and healthier for most dogs. The raised design makes it easier for dogs to eat without bending over, which is especially beneficial for older dogs with arthritis or back problems. Eating from an elevated dish allows dogs to consume their food without swallowing large quantities of air, which they tend to do when they eat from the floor. This reduces gas and cuts down on the risk of bloat.

Canned Foods

Canned foods come in four types: ration, all animal tissue, chunk-style, and stew. The ration foods are ground, cooked into a liquid, and then canned. The animal-tissue foods are not liquefied before canning and may include chunks of identifiable by-products such as arteries. Chunk-style foods are ground and shaped into chunks to disguise the by-products and then covered with gravy before the can is sealed. Stews are designed to please the owner. These budget-priced canned foods all contain ingredients like corn-meal, animal by-products, and lots of water that has been thickened with wheat gluten.

Premium canned dog food is more expensive since it uses human-grade ingredients and a higher percentage of protein with fewer fillers, grains, and preservatives. The best canned food contains chicken, brown rice, barley, and eggs that are free of hormones and chemical preservatives. Like premium dry food, high quality and organic canned foods are available at pet specialty stores, boutiques, and some organic and health food markets.

Canned dog food needs to be refrigerated after opening. Scoop the leftover food out of the original can and store it in a tightly sealed plastic container or bag.

Raw Diet

Although not discussed in this cookbook, many pet nutritionists and pet owners firmly believe that a raw diet comes closest to what dogs and wolves eat in the wild. The diet includes everything from raw chicken, pork, and beef bones to frozen or freeze-dried nuggets that combine meat, fruits, and vegetables. Popular ingredients include beef hearts, broccoli, romaine lettuce, and carrots. Advocates of the raw diet claim it improves periodontal health and can cure everything from arthritis to kidney stones. Critics claim the raw meats carry potentially dangerous bacteria, and the bones pose a choking hazard.

A Dog's Nutritional Needs

The food your dog eats provides the nutrients he needs to promote good health and growth. Essential nutrients include proteins, carbohydrates, fats and oils, minerals, vitamins, and water. Calories should come from healthy foods in an amount that reflects your dog's age, size, lifestyle, and health. Table scraps or people food should not be offered to your dog because the calories they contain can equal the total calories he needs for a whole day. It is up to you to offer your dog a variety of healthy foods..

Proteins

Proteins are necessary for healthy growth and development and should account for a major portion of your dog's diet. Proteins are composed of amino acids, the building blocks required for growth and tissue repair. Amino acids are divided into two groups: essential amino acids and nonessential amino acids. Essential amino acids are those a dog cannot synthesize and therefore must be obtained through his diet. Nonessential amino acids can be synthesized and therefore are not required.

Animal-based proteins are a valuable source of the essential amino acids your dog requires. Chicken, lamb, turkey, beef, and eggs are rich in protein and offer your dog complete amino acid profiles. Fish, vegetables, grains, cheese, and cereals are also high in protein.

 Fact

Dogs need a total of twenty-two amino acids, but their bodies can only synthesize twelve of them. Essential amino acids include arginine, histidine, isoleucine, leucine, lysine, methionine, phenylalanine, threonine, tryptophan, and valine. Good health correlates to the consumption of the proper amino acids.

Carbohydrates

Starches are carbohydrates and are more readily available as an energy source than protein. Carbohydrates create structure, texture, and form in dry dog food. Soluble carbohydrates are found in cereal grains such as rice, wheat, corn, barley, and oats. Some dogs have trouble digesting certain forms of starch, and the symptoms can include excessive gas, bloating, and diarrhea. Wheat and corn products are the biggest culprits; they will affect your dog's digestive system almost immediately. If you constantly monitor what your dog eats, you will have a clearer picture of the types of foods she can tolerate.

Fats

Fats provide your dog with more than twice the energy of proteins or carbohydrates and are the most concentrated source of energy. Fats are essential for good health. They make certain vitamins available for use in the body, cushion vital organs, make up part of all body cells, and help maintain body temperature. As with humans, too much fat can cause health problems such as heart disease, high blood pressure, and diabetes.

Essential fatty acids cannot be synthesized, so they must be part of your dog's diet. Omega-6 and omega-3 fatty acids can reduce the inflammations associated with skin allergies, arthritis, and intestinal disorders. Omega-6 fatty acids are found in fish (such as salmon), whole grains and cereals, most vegetables and vegetable oils, eggs, fruits, and poultry.

Essential

Read the ingredients on your pet's food before you buy it. The sources of fats should come naturally from the ingredients and should not be added as an ingredient. When looking at the Guaranteed Nutritional Analysis on the can, the fat content should be less then 9 percent. Do not purchase canned foods that contain any sort of animal by-products or fillers such as wheat gluten and bone meal.

Minerals

Neither animal nor vegetable, minerals are inorganic. Minerals must be obtained through diet and are vital to keep your dog's body running smoothly. Iron, calcium, and phosphorus are three of the most important minerals. Meat and liver are rich in iron, as are egg yolks and dark green vegetables. Calcium can be found in hard cheeses, leafy greens, nuts, and small fish such as sardines and anchovies. Phosphorus can be found in most foods and works with calcium to strengthen bones and teeth.

Alert!

In pets, hypervitaminosis, poisoning due to ingesting excess vitamins, is actually more common than hypovitaminosis, or vitamin deficiency. This is in part due to the practice of offering vitamin supplements. For dogs, an excess of vitamin A may cause bone and joint pain, brittle bones, and dry skin; too much vitamin D can result in very dense bones or joint calcification. Your veterinarian can determine if your dog is getting the correct amount of vitamins.

Vitamins

Essential for growth and health, most vitamins cannot be manufactured by the body. Vitamins work together with minerals and enzymes to insure normal digestion, reproduction, muscle and bone growth, healthy skin and fur, clotting of blood, and proper use of the fats, proteins, and carbohydrates. There are two groups of vitamins, which are categorized by how the body stores them. Fat-soluble vitamins are stored in the liver and fatty tissue, while water-soluble vitamins are stored in very small amounts and need to be eaten daily. The body excretes excess water-soluble vitamins each day. If your dog eats a well-balanced diet that is partially composed of commercially prepared kibble, you don't need to offer a supplement. If you are preparing all of your dog's food, a vitamin supplement is recommended.

Water

Essential to life, fresh water should be available to your dog at all times. Never let your dog's water bowl go empty, and be sure to really wash it at least once a week. Heavy ceramic bowls are best as they keep water cooler longer and will not tip easily. During the summer, you can add ice cubes to the water bowl to keep the water cool and fresh. Your dog will also probably need to drink more water to keep cool during warmer months.

The more active your dog is, the more water she'll drink. Check her water bowl frequently so that it never ends up dry. After all, it's up to you to provide what she needs. When you travel, whether it is a hike in the woods or a drive to the beach, be sure to bring a bottle of water just for your dog. Some dogs acquire a knack for drinking from pop-up style nozzles, while others prefer a bowl. There are numerous products designed especially for dogs, from collapsible bowls to flask and bowl combinations. If all else fails, you can simply carry a small airtight container.

Foods to Avoid

Dogs and humans have different metabolisms, and some foods that humans can eat are potentially toxic in dogs. Read labels carefully and become familiar with the foods dogs should avoid. After all, you control what your dog eats. Eating the wrong foods may cause mild digestive upsets, but serious reactions include long-term illnesses and even death. Just remember, when in doubt, your dog could probably do without.

Here is a list of the most common foods dogs should avoid:

- **Chocolate:** Chocolate contains theobromine and caffeine. In dogs, chocolate causes increased heart rate, difficulty breathing, vomiting, diarrhea, excessive urination, and restlessness. Toxic doses can lead to seizures, irregular heart rhythm, and even death.

- **Caffeine:** Caffeine is found in coffee, tea, chocolate, cola, and human stimulants. Caffeinated products can be toxic and will affect your dog's heart and nervous system.

- **Grapes and raisins:** Grapes and raisins contain an unknown toxin that can lead to acute kidney and liver failure. The condition is severe and comes on quickly. Some dogs are more susceptible to dangerous effects from grapes and raisins than others, and there is no way to tell unless you encounter a problem.

- **Macadamia nuts:** These fatty nuts contain an unknown toxin that can affect your dog's muscles, as well as her digestive and nervous systems.

- **Mushrooms:** Having your dog avoid eating cultivated mushrooms is easy, but the wild ones that grow on even the best-manicured lawns are a concern. Mushrooms can contain various toxins that can affect your dog's nervous system, causing vomiting and diarrhea.

- **Onions:** Onions and other members of the allium family may cause abnormalities in red blood cells, resulting in anemia.

- **Citrus oil extracts:** Often used in formulating insecticidal sprays, dips, shampoos, insect repellents, food additives, and fragrances, citrus oil extracts can be toxic to both dogs and cats if they are ingested. The most common reaction is vomiting, but drooling and trembling can also indicate that your dog is suffering from a dangerous level of these toxins.

What do I do if my dog was sprayed with citrus oil insect repellent?
Bathe your dog with very warm water and liquid dish soap repeatedly until the citrus smell on his fur is gone. Dry your dog thoroughly and do not allow him to catch a chill. Contact your veterinarian.

Common Food Allergies

Dogs are allergic to some of the very same foods that cause dangerous reactions in humans, including peanuts, wheat, and dairy products. Corn, beef, chicken, eggs, and fish are also on the short list of common canine allergies. Itchy, flaky skin is one of the most common symptoms of a food allergy, and dogs that scratch excessively or bite their feet and legs may be trying to alleviate the discomfort caused by food allergies. Irritated ears and diarrhea are other possible signs to be on the lookout for. However, these symptoms are indicative of many other conditions, so it is important to consult with your veterinarian for a positive diagnosis.

 *Fact*

Allergies can develop over time after dogs have been continuously exposed to foods. Even dogs that are well into adulthood may develop new allergies to common foods they never had problems with before.

If your veterinarian determines food allergies are a potential cause of your dog's discomfort, she can help you determine which foods are the culprits and recommend healthy alternatives. To find out which foods your dog is allergic to, your veterinarian may place him on a highly restrictive diet encompassing meals, treats, medications, and even toys. This diet may last as long as four months to allow your veterinarian to track results. Suspected foods are individually added back into your dog's diet to see whether symptoms will reappear.

Dogs with food allergies can eat specially formulated food, either commercially manufactured or homemade. Making your own food allows you the flexibility of tailoring recipes to your dog's unique needs, and although many of the recipes in this book contain foods your dog may be allergic to, there are also suggestions for substitutions for the offending ingredients.

Generally, you can substitute different types of meat if your dog is allergic to specific meats. For instance, if the recipe for Sauerbraten sounds good to you but your dog is allergic to beef, substitute lamb or chicken for the beef and use chicken or vegetable broth instead of beef broth. In the baking recipes, use rice flour or oat flour if your dog is allergic to wheat or corn, but you may need to experiment with the proportions to get the right consistency.

Food intolerances are different from food allergies. Food intolerance symptoms can include upset stomach and diarrhea and can be easily remedied by eliminating the offending foods from your dog's diet.

Weight Control

In a January 2007 press release approving a weight loss drug for dogs, the Food and Drug Administration cited surveys that found 25–35 percent of U.S. dogs are overweight or obese. Managing your dog's weight is not just under your control; it is your responsibility as an owner. Obesity can lead to many health issues including diabetes, back problems, lethargy, heart disease, high blood pressure, increased heat intolerance, and digestive disorders. Additionally, overweight dogs may suffer joint, bone, and ligament damage from carrying around extra pounds. Breeds with long backs—dachshunds, corgis, basset hounds, and even Pekingese—are more prone to back problems if they are overweight.

Aside from noticing your dog's collar has gotten too tight, the easiest way to determine whether your dog is carrying excess weight is by feeling for her ribs. You should be able to feel them quite easily, even with a slight amount of fat covering them. If you can't feel her ribs, your dog is overweight. Another easy test is to look at your dog from above. Your dog should have a defined waist behind her ribs, and her hips should not be as wide as her chest.

To begin a weight-loss program for your dog, you should first consult your veterinarian. He will be able to help you understand the process and time it will take for your dog to lose the weight. Carefully restricting what and when your dog eats are the first steps in weight control. If your dog continues to eat her current food, the daily intake should be reduced according to your veterinarian's suggestions. A dry kibble that is lower in fat will allow you to feed your dog the same amount of food without as many calories. Feeding your dog smaller meals more often and feeding her away from other members of the family is also helpful. Healthy snacks such as carrots, broccoli, and cooked green beans can be offered between meals. Dogs lose weight slowly, so it will take about three months of constant vigilance to see a 15 percent weight loss.

 **Alert!**

While it's normal for dogs to add a few pounds as they age, significant weight gain—especially over a short period—may be a sign of an underlying health problem such as thyroid disease. Check with your veterinarian just to be sure.

Daily exercise is also important. Exercise is good for the heart, and your dog will have more energy, feel younger, and be livelier with regular exercise. If your dog isn't used to much exertion, consult your veterinarian and start slowly. Eventually you'll be able to build up to long, brisk walks or even jogs, depending on your dog's breed. Your dog will live longer, and you will enjoy the company of a happier and healthier pet.

Feeding Your Dog the Smart Way

If you find it impossible to resist the temptation to sneak your dog a small tidbit from your plate, you are not alone. However, consider these facts the next time the urge strikes you. If you reward begging behavior with table scraps even once, you can be certain your dog will be at your side every time you sit down to a meal. Table scraps do not supply the proper nutrition dogs require, and the more you offer your food, the less likely he will be willing to eat his own. By feeding your dog table scraps you are simply filling him with empty calories, and the habit can lead to weight and health problems as well as digestive disorders. Your dog can end up suffering from bad breath, gas, and loose stool. Finally, dogs that are used to eating people food will be more inclined to sift through garbage bags and even try stealing from the table.

Believe it or not, dog biscuits are the better choice when you want to reward your dog. Whether you purchase biscuits or bake your own, quality treats are more nutritious and tend to have fewer calories than most table scraps. Steer clear of treats that contain high amounts of sugar and fat and remember to offer treats in moderation. They should never amount to more than 10 percent of your dog's daily food intake.

 Essential

To determine which treats should you buy, read the list of ingredients and make your selection based on what you find. If the second ingredient is a form of sugar, your dog does not need it no matter how pretty or cute the biscuits look. Although it goes by many names, sugar is still sugar, whether it's listed as honey, molasses, corn syrup, brown rice syrup, or raw sugar.

There are many different kinds of treats for your dog to enjoy, and dogs appreciate variation in their diets just as much as their owners do.

- Biscuits or other larger treats can be awarded to a dog that has behaved well—for example, a dog that reacted calmly when your pizza was delivered. An added benefit of eating hard biscuits is that they are good for your dog's teeth and gums.
- Small, tasty training treats are excellent for helping your dog master desirable behaviors. Since these treats are so tiny, you won't lose your dog's attention while she eats her reward. Training sessions will run more smoothly for both of you.
- Treat-dispensing toys make your dog work for his snacks. These are ideal for providing your dog with mental stimulation. Toys can be filled with kibble, small treats, or even natural peanut butter. It is best to watch your dog the first time you give him a filled toy. If he becomes frustrated and angry, take the toy away, as he is not having fun.

Keep in mind that your dog's dietary needs and preferences will change as she gets older.

Chapter 2

Canine Culinary Basics

Dogs will eat almost anything. It's up to their owners to make choices that are smart, healthy, and nutritious. Chapter 1 covered what you should and shouldn't feed your dog; this chapter is all about what materials you need to make an enjoyable treat for him.

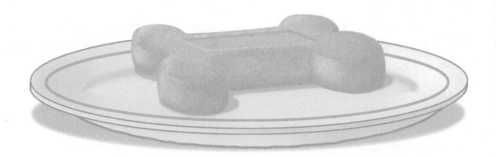

Getting Started

Before deciding on a particular recipe, review the ingredients and consider what you know your dog likes and what she can tolerate. If your dog loves cheese, consider starting with the Chopped Spinach and Cheddar Cheese Biscuits on page 38 or the Swiss Cheese on Rye Biscuits found on page 52. Dogs that must refrain from eating wheat, corn, and gluten can be offered any of the biscuits from Chapter 4. Even if your dog seems to be able to stomach anything, introduce a new food slowly in small amounts, checking to make sure it agrees with her digestive system.

Unlike their human counterparts, dogs are very forgiving. Perhaps the biscuits aren't cut perfectly or the stew looks like gruel, but if it smells right, your dog will happily taste your culinary endeavors. You will be able to enjoy the satisfaction that comes from preparing a meal for your loved ones.

On Baking Biscuits

Baking biscuits for your dog is perhaps the easiest place to begin. All the recipes start with a base of flour and fat, with the addition of fruit, vegetables, and/or meats. Baking rolled biscuits is a fun family activity, and the advantage of baking dog biscuits is that you never have to worry about overworking the dough. The trick is to form a dough that has a nice smooth consistency. If it's too sticky or too stiff, the problem is easily remedied by adding a pinch of flour or a bit more liquid. As you continue to bake, you will begin to get the "feel" of the dough and know the right proportions instinctively.

Rolling dough may seem intimidating at first, but all you need to do is roll it to an even thickness. To cut shapes more easily, dip a cookie cutter in flour and gently tap off the extra flour. This will help the biscuits separate from the cookie cutter and the surrounding dough. If you're getting the family involved or want to experiment with different shapes, keep in mind it's best for everyone to work with the same size cookie cutter so that the baking time is consistent for all the biscuits on a cookie sheet.

If you are fortunate enough to have a convection oven, the oven's ability to maintain the correct temperature and constantly circulate the heat will fully dry your biscuits. This is important because moisture is the culprit behind moldy biscuits. Adding too much fat will cause biscuits to go rancid, and improper storage will cause the biscuits to go stale. These facts are mentioned not to alarm or discourage you, but to explain why a homemade dog biscuit may not be the same texture or consistency as commercially baked biscuits. If stored in a tin and eaten in a timely manner, your dog will have the pleasure of eating healthy and flavorful biscuits.

 Essential

Make your dog's biscuits special. Use cookie cutters to cut them into bones or other fun shapes. Take advantage of the size differences in cookie cutters to make teeny-tiny biscuits for toy dogs and huge biscuits for giant breeds.

On Baking Cakes

If you are planning your dog's birthday party and want to bake him a cake, you can create a simple, fun, and healthy cake with just a little planning. Sugar and salt are not required, nor should they even be included when preparing cake batter for a dog. The addition of cooked meats or chopped vegetables may not agree with your palate, but it will please your four-legged guests. Portions should be kept small and preferably served outdoors to avoid a mess on your floors or rugs. Feeding all the guests their cake at the same time makes a great photo opportunity if you can catch them all with their heads down, gobbling up your confection!

If you bake some biscuits in assorted shapes, you can arrange them on top of the icing as decorations. Whether the biscuits spell your dog's name or are cut in the shape of flowers, stars, or varying sized circles, the important thing is to remember that a home-baked cake contains ingredients that are dog friendly. Your dog and her friends will be very forgiving if the cake is lopsided or suffers from other aesthetic imperfections. Their main concern is the taste, and your main concern should be the ingredients.

 *Fact*

Traditional birthday party etiquette states that guests should bring a present for the birthday celebrant. It is therefore quite appropiate and will be greatly appreciated when you send your guests home with a gift bag as you would for a child's birthday party.

There are many "gourmet" and designer biscuits and cakes available that emulate human-style desserts, from cannolis to iced cookies to doughnuts. Many of these products are made with a yogurt product that actually contains sugar, and the sprinkles atop the "cookies" are the same you would use on your own ice-cream cones or cupcakes. Since many of these items are sold from bakery cases, the easiest way to determine whether these products contain sugar is by smelling them. If it smells sweet and you would consider taking a nibble, then the odds are your dog could do without it. Sugar can lead to diabetes and weight problems. Just because a food item is produced and sold does not mean that it is healthy or good for your dog.

On Cooking Meals

The main meal recipes in this book are meant to supplement—not replace—what you currently feed your dog. If you start with a high-quality kibble, preferably one that is organic, low in fat, and high in fiber, you can vary your dog's meals quite simply. For every half cup of kibble you normally feed your dog, add one serving of your homemade food.

If you are organized and plan your family dinner weekly, you can put aside a portion of the main ingredient and find a recipe that also suits your dog. You can freeze small portions in ice-cube trays and store them in resealable plastic bags. If you have a microwave-safe dog bowl, you can defrost the "meal cubes" in the microwave. Add the kibble after the cubes are defrosted and thinned to the desired consistency. Don't microwave the kibble; it needs to be crunchy to maintain healthy teeth and oral hygiene.

The Essential Pantry

Before you begin, you should stock up on the common ingredients recommended for creating healthy, flavorful, and nutritious biscuits, treats, and meals for your dog. You may cook for yourself and may already have these items in your kitchen. The ingredients listed here are readily available at your local grocery or can be purchased from specialty Web sites listed in Appendix A.

The opinion on the dietary use of garlic for dogs is strongly divided. Garlic is a member of the allium family. Like onions, garlic can trigger Heinz body anemia and may prove toxic to sensitive dogs. While garlic is used extensively in the recipes in this cookbook, the publisher and author recommend consulting a veterinarian should you have any concerns or questions about feeding garlic to your dog.

Fresh Garlic

Garlic is used extensively to impart an aromatic flavor when sautéed in olive oil. Select bulbs that are firm and whose cloves are tightly packed. Garlic contains vitamin C and is thought to regulate blood sugar levels, fight infections, and help digestive disorders. Popular throughout ancient times, garlic was consumed by the Egyptians, the Greeks, and the Romans. Its power to repel vampires and protect against the Evil Eye is legendary.

Natural Unsalted Peanut Butter

High in protein, peanut butter is a favorite food for dogs and kids. Select a brand that does not contain sugar or salt. You will taste the difference in pure peanut butter, and your dog will be healthier. Peanut butter is used in many recipes in this book because it is relatively inexpensive, found in nearly every American kitchen cabinet, and offers flavor and fiber. As an added bonus, its calories are converted into pure energy.

Oils

Dogs, like humans, need fats in their diets, and oils are a prime source of fats. Fats are essential to keep the body well oiled and running smoothly, but they should be eaten in moderation. Overconsumption of fats contributes to weight gain, heart disease, and certain types of cancer. There are "good fats" and "bad fats." Most good fats occur naturally in oils, nuts, or other foods. They lower bad cholesterol levels and raise good cholesterol levels. Peanuts, peanut oil, olive oil, and canola oil are all sources of good fats. Bad fats are found in animal meats and processed foods, and they raise bad cholesterol levels.

Virgin Olive Oil

While Italian olive oil is most commonly available, very good oil also comes from Spain and Greece. Virgin olive oil is heavier than other vegetable oils, so use it sparingly because it thins during heating. Olive oil in particular will improve your dog's coat without adding to his waistline.

Fact

The term virgin means that the oil was produced without any chemical treatment. Olive oil is tagged as the healthy oil, but be wary of potentially misleading labels. Just because an olive oil is called "light" does not mean a lower fat content. Rather, it is lighter in color and lacks taste.

Canola Oil

Canola oil is another healthy oil and is preferred over vegetable or corn oil. The most common of all cooking oils, canola oil is low in bad fats and contains good fats. Canola oil is used throughout the recipes, replacing the ingredient you would most likely use if you were making the recipes on your own—butter. Fats are required and necessary when preparing baked products, but this cookbook takes advantage of good fats to avoid health problems for your dog.

Flaxseed Oil

While flaxseed oil has been around a long time, it has recently gained popularity since it contains good fats. Flaxseed oil also contains vitamin B and potassium, and it can benefit the cardiovascular system, the immune system, joints, and the nervous system. Flaxseed oil should be used sparingly as it tends to go rancid quickly, can be pricey, and requires refrigeration to help extend its life. If you wanted to add flaxseed oil to any of the recipes, replace one tablespoon of canola oil with flaxseed oil. Too much flaxseed oil can lead to loose stool and upset stomach, so keep a record of how well your dog can handle flaxseed.

Flours

There are many types of flours available on the market today, and you are no longer limited to bleached white flour. In fact, bleached white flour contains a harmful chemical called alloxan. Alloxan is used to make white flour look clean and pure, but it can actually lead to the destruction of beta cells in the pancreas and increase the risk of diabetes. Unbleached flour should be your first choice for all your baking endeavors, whether for your dog or yourself.

Whole-Wheat Flour

A more flavorful and nutritious choice, wheat flour is made from grinding the entire wheat grain. Many of the recipes in this cookbook call for whole-wheat flour. Using whole-wheat flour exclusively will result in a heavier and denser product, but you can combine it with other flours for a lighter taste. Once opened, whole-wheat flour should be stored in the refrigerator.

All wheat flours contain gluten, the proteins that create the elasticity in dough. Some dogs are allergic to gluten and require a diet without wheat or products that contain gluten. Allergic reactions can include diarrhea, vomiting, and gas. Flours that do not contain gluten include rice flours, cornmeal, quinoa, buckwheat flour, amaranth, and oats. Working with flours that lack gluten can be tricky; the dough crumbles easily and its texture and feel is more like sand. To help overcome these difficulties, biscuit recipes using gluten-free flours are assembled in Chapter 4 as refrigerator biscuits, rather than as rolled biscuits.

Rice Flour

Rice flour is gluten-free and is the preferred flour when preparing biscuits for dogs with allergies. Store rice flour in the refrigerator in a resealable bag. Rice flour will create a light and crisp biscuit that will break easily but will not crumble. The taste is mild; brown rice flour tastes slightly nutty.

Barley Flour

Low in fat and gluten, barley flour has a mild roasted-grain aroma and a bland taste. It is often suggested as a grain substitution for dogs with allergies, but it does contain gluten. Barley flour can also be used as a thickener when creating a roux or used for flouring meats, poultry, or fish. Store barley flour in the refrigerator in a resealable plastic bag.

Old-Fashioned Rolled Oats

Rolled oats are actually the cleaned, hulled, and toasted oat grains of oat groats that have been steamed and flattened with a steel roller. Oats offer a nutty flavor and a nice texture, and they're good for the digestive system. While placed on the shelf next to "quick" or "instant" oatmeal, be sure to select the box that is labeled "Old-Fashioned Rolled Oats." Old-fashioned oats are higher in dietary fiber and are filled with cholesterol-fighting soluble fiber. Rolled oats can be made into flour by processing them in a food processor.

Cheese

Cheese is one of the oldest foods in the world and is truly versatile in the kitchen. Cheese adds flavor and aroma and is rich in calcium. Organic cheeses are manufactured from the milk of animals that weren't injected with hormones or antibiotics or fed food that contained animal by-products or pesticides.

Fact

Dogs can usually enjoy cheese and other dairy products in small amounts, but many dogs suffer from lactose intolerance as they get older. This is a condition in which the body does not manufacture enough of the enzyme lactase needed for proper digestion of lactose, the sugars found in dairy products. The most common symptoms are excessive gas, stomachache, and diarrhea. Monitor your dog's intake of dairy products to determine whether she can handle them.

Pecorino Romano

Made of sheep's milk, Romano cheese is the perfect hard Italian grating cheese. Select a piece that is aged at least eight months. Keep the cheese wrapped in plastic wrap and stored in a resealable bag in the refrigerator. Grate only what you need. Stored grated cheese will lose its flavor and even become stale. Never buy cheese that is pregrated or comes in a box or can.

Organic Cheddar Cheese

Cheddar cheese is a firm-textured, semihard cheese with a rich, nutty flavor. It is one of the most popular of all cheeses. Its mildness or sharpness is determined by the amount of time it is aged. Cheddar is a good source of protein and calcium and most dogs love it. While most organic cheeses are white in color, annatto seeds can be ground to a powder and used to provide a natural source of color.

Organic Meat and Vegetable Broths

Using broths rather than water is a good, simple way to add flavor to any recipe. Look for broth that is packaged in resealable aseptic cartons and does not contain monosodium glutamate (MSG), sulfites, or excessive amounts of salt. The resealable aseptic carton allows the broth to be stored in the refrigerator for up to ten days. Organic chicken broth can be expensive, but many specialty grocery stores often put it on sale, and some warehouse stores carry it packed by the case.

Nitrate-Free Bacon

Bacon is the cut of meat taken from the sides, back, or belly of a pig and subsequently cured and smoked. Today, turkey and chicken bacon are also available for consumers who want a leaner, lower-calorie alternative. Bacon can be grilled, baked in the oven, or cooked in the microwave. Crisp bacon crumbles easily and adds an intense smoky flavor that dogs love. Avoid using bacon that contains nitrates and nitrites, antibiotics, and other chemicals, all of which are unnecessary and contain cancer-causing agents.

Applegate Farms produces bacon, sausage, and various other cold cuts without adding chemical preservatives. Instead, Applegate starts with antibiotic-free meats and captures the flavor of old-fashioned country bacon. Their goal is to create the perfect balance between good taste and healthy living.

The Benefits of Organic

As people become more aware of the foods they eat and the process in which foods are grown and manufactured, current food trends show a surge in the popularity of organic foods. Although organic fruits and vegetables are now commonplace, many natural and socially responsible manufacturing companies offer consumers organic products that include everything from frozen pizza and yogurt to dog biscuits!

Sales of organic pet foods are growing at a rate nearly three times the rate of organic human food. These premium products can cost up to twice as much as the "supermarket" variety. Organic pet foods are minimally processed and they do not include some troubling ingredients that the Association of American Feed Control Officials (AAFCO) finds acceptable for the production of commercial dog and cat food. Believe it or not, the AAFCO allows ingredients such as hair, blood, waste, and "animal meal."

U.S. Department of Agriculture guidelines mandate organic food must be grown and processed without conventional chemical pesticides, herbicides, or fertilizers. Animals used in organic food products may not be enhanced with hormones or genetic engineering. In order to display the "USDA Organic" stamp, at least 95 percent of the ingredients used must be organic. Organic products are also good for the environment as streams, rivers, lakes, groundwater, and wildlife are not compromised by harmful chemicals. Healthy foods are grown in healthy soil, so you can see, taste, and smell the difference.

Dogs' bodies are smaller than ours and if we can offer them food that is free of preservatives, additives, and artificial colors and flavors, they will be healthier and happier and will perhaps live longer.

Basic Kitchen Tools

Although you may already own most of the tools recommended here, remember a tool that is well crafted will allow you to be more successful in all your baking and cooking endeavors and will help make the process easier and more efficient.

 *Essential*

Remember to allow baked goods to cool slightly in their original pan before transferring them to cooling racks. Do not place racks on a wooden table; the steam from the baked product will damage the table, leaving a white film. Wash the racks with hot soapy water, but do not scrub too much or you will remove the protective coating.

Here is a list of essential kitchen tools:

Electric mixer: KitchenAid mixers are perhaps the best overall tabletop mixer available to the home cook. A versatile appliance, the KitchenAid ten-speed mixer comes with a five-quart bowl, wire whisk, flat beater, and dough hook. Available in a variety of colors and price ranges, its all-metal construction offers years of dependable service.

Food processor: Whether you have a processor with a three-cup capacity or a three-quart capacity, this handy machine allows you to quickly and easily chop, mince, blend, mix, and emulsify foods.

Balloon whisk: Made with stainless steel or silicone, whisks are as great for combining dry ingredients as they are for beating wet ingredients.

Parchment paper: Used to line cookie sheets and cake pans, parchment paper requires no greasing and easily releases all baked goods that would otherwise stick to cooking surfaces. Parchment paper is coated with silicone so it will not burn in the oven; the surface also helps distribute heat evenly across the cookie sheet or cake pan. Available in rolls or precut sheets, parchment paper can be purchased bleached or unbleached. One sheet of parchment paper can be reused several times, so save it until it's truly ready to be thrown away.

Two-cup glass measuring cup: Made of heat-resistant glass, the two-cup measuring cup is a convenient "bowl" that allows you to measure and mix wet ingredients at the same time. Hard to break and easy to clean, the glass can be placed in the dishwasher and is perfect for the microwave when you need to heat or melt ingredients. It's also the perfect size vessel for beating eggs.

A standard bridal shower gift, the one- or two-cup glass measuring cup is a timeless kitchen tool. Although it's possible to survive with only measuring cups for dry ingredients, it's not recommended. A one-cup dry measuring cup holds exactly one cup, and you'll inevitably slosh liquid over the side as you transfer it from the carton to the mixing bowl. A liquid measuring cup gives you more leeway, and you can combine several wet ingredients before adding them all at once to your recipe

Bakeware: Cookie sheets and cake pans are essential for fixing delectable treats. Consider buying at least two cookie sheets and two cake pans. Duplicates will allow you to prepare one sheet or pan while the other is in the oven. Parchment paper makes the nonstick-coating options irrelevant, but generally the heavier the item, the better able to withstand high heat and regular use for many years. The same applies to cookware

Cookware: Casserole dishes and pots and pans are all kitchen staples. Products that conduct heat well will help you quickly and efficiently prepare food.

Cooling racks: Transfer baked goods from cookie sheets or cake pans to cooling racks to economize on space and to cool biscuits quickly and correctly. Available in various sizes, select the largest you can store and accommodate on your counters. Stackable racks are ideal for kitchens with minimal counter space. The aluminized steel grid rack allows biscuits, cookies, and cakes to cool properly and prevents "sweating." Sweating occurs when a baked cake is left in its pan too long. The steam creates moisture, which cannot escape and collects in the form of sweat. This can result in a cake with a soft or mushy bottom

Resealable plastic bags: These convenient bags are perfect for storing everything from dry ingredients to uncooked meats and vegetables. Select the size and closure method that suits your needs.

Essential Biscuit-Baking Tools

While the actual baking process is based on chemistry and the correct combination and proportions of ingredients, your kitchen drawers and cabinets hold many versatile tools that can help you make better biscuits. Do not be afraid to work with what you have and be creative—use a pastry wheel to cut simple shapes, a two-pronged fork to create "button" holes, and a glass to cut circles. Working with dough is one of life's simple pleasures; it's both relaxing and comforting at the same time. Experiment with it and don't worry about making mistakes.

Essential

Once you start baking, you will find yourself collecting cookie cutters. Many people feel nostalgic about cookie cutters and remember a certain shape that reminds them of a special holiday, recipe, or person. It will be easier to remember what you have if you keep a list of your cookie cutters, defined by shape and size.

Here is a list of the essential tools you'll need for treats that look and taste great

Cookie cutters: Made of plastic, stainless steel, or copper, cookie cutters are available in almost any shape or size. Use any size cutter you want, but remember to use the same size for each batch to keep baking times consistent.

Cookie sheets: Measure the interior size of your oven and purchase the largest size cookie sheet that will fit. Make sure the cookie sheets are crafted of heavy gauge aluminized steel, resist warping, and allow for even heat distribution.

Wooden rolling pin: The key to successful and easy dough rolling, a well-crafted rolling pin is truly your most essential tool.

Hand-held cheese grater: This versatile tool allows you to grate, shred, or shave cheese, lemon, or orange peel evenly and quickly.

Pizza wheel: Select a pizza wheel that fits comfortably in your hand and provides a good grip.

When selecting a rolling pin, choose a heavy one. The weight makes rolling easier and means you'll be able to shape your dough efficiently. Rolling pins are available in a variety of materials including marble and stainless steel, but wood is the most commonly used substance.

Essential Cake-Baking Tools

With so many stores and catalog companies claiming to be the place for cooking tools, it is easy to wonder whether the cost of these designer bakeware products is really necessary. The long and short answer is a resounding yes! Purchasing professional and commercial-grade basics are worth the investment. They are built to last, constructed to insure even baking, and readily available at nearby stores and online. What you don't need are fancy tools you will only use once. While these gadgets are fun and tempting, you can improvise with something you already have in your kitchen and no one will know the difference.

Here is a list of the essential tools you'll need for baking cakes:

Cake pans: Available in assorted shapes and sizes, purchase two pans the same size. Most cake recipes call for eight-inch pans, but that doesn't mean the pan has to be round! Cakes baked in square pans are easy to decorate and receive unexpected adulation

Offset spatula: Thin and flexible, the offset spatula's stainless steel blade allows you to apply frosting smoothly across a cake's surface

Silicon spoon spatula: This is the ideal tool for blending and folding ingredients or just scraping a bowl clean. Today most spatulas are made of silicon, so they won't crack, stain, or absorb flavors. The head of the spatula is removable for cleaning, and you can select from a range of colors, sizes, and shapes.

Professional food coloring: Whether you select liquid, powder, or paste, professional food coloring offers an intense color palette for you to work with. When trying to decide what color food coloring to buy, remember you can easily mix colors to achieve the desired color and shade. Your basic selection should include the primary colors: red, yellow, blue, and black. From these, you can mix any other color you desire. In cake decorating, the base icing is your white paint.

Pastry bag: There are many sizes and styles of pastry bags. Select a cloth bag lined with polyethylene. The interior plastic coating allows for easy cleaning, and the outside fabric never gets slippery

Pastry tips: Often sold by the set, stainless-steel or plastic pastry tips can also be purchased separately. Basic sets include varying sizes of round and star-shaped tips, as well as tips used for basket-weave, rose, and leaf decoration.

If you decide to purchase pastry bags and tips separately, you will also need a plastic coupler. The coupler is a two-piece unit that fits the pastry tip to the pastry bag.

Question?

Why don't cake layers line up at home as they do in bakeries?
Unlike the cake pans available to the home cook, professional cake pans have straight sides and reinforced rims. Commercial-quality cake pans are constructed of heavy-gauge aluminized steel to ensure even baking.

How to Use This Book

The recipes in this cookbook yield enough to feed multiple dogs or last for several days. This is ideal if you have more than one dog or are hosting a party. Leftovers can always be refrigerated and used later in the week or frozen and stored for longer periods.

Here is a general list of how much each recipe yields and how much you should feed your dog:

Biscuits: All biscuit recipes yield about thirty 2-inch biscuits.

Biscotti: All biscotti recipes yield about 100 crouton-size biscotti.

Training treats: All training treat recipes yield about 1 cup of small crumbles and bite-size bits.

Meals and flavor enhancers: Meals and sauces are meant to be served over kibble. Give your dog one serving of homemade food for each half-cup of kibble. The poultry and meat recipes yield many small servings, while the egg and seafood recipes yield a few larger servings.

Party food: All snack food and cake recipes are just right for entertaining groups of dogs. Send your guests home with doggie bags of leftovers—if there are any!

For the most part, the ingredients in this cookbook were selected because they are easy to use and easy to find. You may already have many of these ingredients in your kitchen because you use them to cook and bake for yourself. Some recipes require more uncommon ingredients. These are perfect if you want to prepare a special meal or treat for your dog or if you've experimented with some of the ingredients in a fancy dish for yourself and have leftovers.

There are four icons in this book designed to help you choose the right meals for your dog.

 Look for this icon if your dog is allergic to **wheat and gluten**. The recipes with this icon do not contain wheat or gluten. All of the recipes in Chapter 4 use wheat substitutes and are good for dogs with allergies.

 Recipes with this icon are good for dogs with **sensitive stomachs.** Think about making these recipes if your dog has had an upset tummy or if you want to offer something gentle.

 This icon is a guideline for owners whose dogs are **on diets.** Your dog can have healthy food that still tastes good.

 If you don't have much time, whip up one of these **quick and easy** recipes. The timer denotes speed and ease of preparation.

Chapter 3

Hand-Rolled Biscuits

Peanut Butter, Carrot, and Wheat Germ Biscuits

Carrot and peanut butter biscuits combine two flavors dogs love.
For added crunch and texture, use chunky-style peanut butter.

Yields 30 biscuits

1 cup unbleached flour
½ cup whole-wheat flour
½ cup unflavored wheat germ
2 teaspoons baking powder
½ cup unsalted natural
*   peanut butter*
¼ cup grated carrot
½ cup filtered water

Natural Peanut Butter

Many popular brands of peanut butter contain high amounts of sugar and salt. Natural peanut butter is simply ground, roasted, and blended peanuts without any artificial sweeteners, artificial colors, or preservatives. Peanut butter is a common ingredient for many dog biscuit recipes so it is important to use the best quality you can find.

1. Preheat the oven to 325°F.
2. Measure the unbleached flour, whole-wheat flour, wheat germ, and baking powder into a mixing bowl. Whisk until combined.
3. Combine the peanut butter, carrot, and water in a glass measuring cup. Stir with a fork until smooth and creamy.
4. Make a well in the flour, and pour in the peanut butter mixture. Mix on medium speed using a paddle attachment until combined.
5. Turn the dough out onto a slightly floured surface and gently knead until dough is smooth and still soft. Roll dough ¼-inch thick and cut biscuits into desired shapes with cookie cutters.
6. Place biscuits on a parchment-lined cookie sheet and bake 12–15 minutes until dry and firm to the touch. Turn the oven off and leave biscuits in another 20–30 minutes. Remove them from the oven, cool them on a baking rack, and store them in a cookie tin.

Banana Cinnamon Biscuits

Here is a good way to avoid wasting those overripe bananas sitting on the counter. Do not store bananas in a bag, and never refrigerate them.

1. Preheat the oven to 325°F.
2. Measure the unbleached flour, whole-wheat flour, baking powder, and cinnamon into a mixing bowl. Whisk until combined.
3. Combine the mashed banana, peanut butter, carrot, and water in a glass measuring cup. Stir with a fork till smooth and creamy.
4. Make a well in the flour, and pour in the banana–peanut butter mixture. Mix on medium speed using a paddle attachment until combined.
5. Turn the dough out onto a slightly floured surface and gently knead until dough is smooth and still soft. Roll the dough ¼-inch thick and cut the biscuits into desired shapes with cookie cutters.
6. Place the biscuits on a parchment-lined cookie sheet and bake 12–15 minutes till dry and firm to the touch. Turn the oven off and leave biscuits in another 20–30 minutes. Remove them from the oven, cool them on a baking rack, and store them in a cookie tin.

Yields 30 biscuits

1 cup unbleached flour
1 cup whole-wheat flour
2 teaspoons baking powder
1 teaspoon cinnamon
1 ripe banana, mashed
¼ cup natural unsalted
   peanut butter
¼ cup grated carrot
½ cup filtered water

Bananas

Bananas are the world's most popular fruit. Nearly 400 varieties are grown in 132 countries. The average American eats twenty-seven pounds of them every year. Bananas are naturally fat-free, contain vitamins and fiber, taste good, and are a great source of energy. Available in a variety of sizes and colors ranging from yellow to red and even purple, bananas may be eaten raw or cooked. Bananas can also be dried and ground into a flour.

Barbecued Chicken in a Biscuit

Be sure to read the ingredients on bottled barbecue sauces before you purchase them. Avoid sauces that contain MSG and are too high in salt or sugar.

Yields 30 biscuits

1 cup unbleached flour
1 cup rolled oats
2 teaspoons baking powder
1 chicken breast, cut into thick slices
2 teaspoons virgin olive oil
2 tablespoons barbecue sauce
½ cup organic free-range chicken broth
4 tablespoons canola oil

MSG

Developed in Japan in the early 1900s, monosodium glutamate is a food additive, marketed as a "flavor enhancer." Today, MSG is found in most canned soups, most beef and chicken stocks, flavored chips, and other snack foods and instant meals. Allergic symptoms include facial pressure or tightness, headache, chest pain, tingling, numbness, and—in extreme cases—difficulty breathing.

1. Preheat the oven to 325°F.
2. Measure the flour, oats, and baking powder into a mixing bowl and whisk together.
3. Heat a grill pan over medium heat. Toss the sliced chicken breast in the virgin olive oil and place on the hot grill. Cook chicken on both sides. Remove the chicken to a plate and toss with 1 tablespoon barbecue sauce. Allow to cool.
4. Pour the chicken broth into the grill pan and scrape up the brown bits. Transfer liquid into a glass measuring cup. Add the canola oil. Pulse the chicken in a food processor. Add the coarsely chopped chicken to the broth and stir.
5. Make a well in the flour, and pour in the chicken mixture. Mix on medium speed using a paddle attachment until combined.
6. Turn the dough out onto a slightly floured surface and gently knead. Roll the dough until it is ¼-inch thick; cut the biscuits into desired shapes with cookie cutters.
7. Place the biscuits on a parchment-lined cookie sheet and bake 12 to 15 minutes.
8. Remove the cookie sheet from oven, and baste the biscuits with the remaining tablespoon of barbecue sauce. Turn the oven off and leave biscuits in another 20–30 minutes. Remove them from oven, cool them on a baking rack, and store them in a cookie tin. Keep refrigerated, and use the biscuits within one week.

Green Apple and Turkey Sausage Biscuits

Use only freshly made, all-natural, preservative-free sausage for this recipe. If you are lucky enough to have a farmer's market nearby, buy your sausage in bulk. That way, it will already be out of the casing.

Yields 30 biscuits

2 teaspoons virgin olive oil
3 cloves garlic, chopped
¼ pound sweet Italian turkey sausage
1 cup unbleached flour
1 cup rolled oats
2 teaspoons baking powder
½ green apple, coarsely chopped
½ cup organic free-range chicken broth

1. In a small skillet, heat the olive oil and sauté the garlic over low heat. Remove the sausage casing and add the sausage meat to the skillet. Use a wooden spoon to break sausage apart into little crumbles. Cook till sausage bits are browned and nearly crunchy. Remove from heat and allow to cool.
2. Preheat the oven to 325°F.
3. Whisk the flour, rolled oats, and baking powder together in a mixing bowl.
4. Empty the sausage bits, garlic, and oil into a glass measuring cup. Add the chopped apple. Pour the chicken broth into the pan and scrape up the brown bits. Pour the chicken broth and bits into the apple-sausage mixture. Stir with a fork until combined.
5. Make a well in the flour and pour in the sausage mixture. Mix on medium speed using a paddle attachment.
6. Turn the dough out onto a slightly floured surface and gently knead. Roll the dough ¼-inch thick, and cut the biscuits into desired shapes with cookie cutters.
7. Place the biscuits on a parchment-lined cookie sheet and bake 12–15 minutes. Turn the oven off and leave the biscuits in another 20–30 minutes. Remove them from oven, cool them on a baking rack, and store them in a cookie tin.

Chopped Spinach and Cheddar Cheese Biscuits

Spinach and cheese have a natural affinity for each other. Dogs love cheese, and using it to flavor spinach biscuits is the healthier and smarter way to offer this treat.

Yields 30 biscuits

1 cup unbleached flour
1 cup rolled oats
2 teaspoons baking powder
½ cup natural Cheddar cheese, grated
½ cup chopped frozen spinach
4 tablespoons canola oil
½ cup filtered water

Cheese-Grating Shortcuts

For variety, you can purchase several flavors of mild hard cheeses and create your own cheese blends. Cut the cheeses into chunks, place them into a food processor with several tablespoons of flour, and process till finely ground. Store the cheese blend in resealable plastic bags in the freezer for up to three months. Simply remove the amount of cheese you require and use as is.

1. Preheat the oven to 325°F.
2. Measure the flour, rolled oats, and baking powder into a mixing bowl and whisk till combined. Add the grated cheese.
3. Squeeze any excess water from the spinach and add the spinach to the flour mixture. Stir with a fork until combined.
4. Make a well in the flour and add the canola oil. Mix on medium speed using a paddle attachment till crumbly. Add the water all at once and mix till dough forms and all ingredients are combined.
5. Turn the dough out onto a slightly floured surface and gently knead until dough is smooth and soft. Roll the dough ¼-inch thick, and cut the biscuits into desired shapes with cookie cutters.
6. Place the biscuits on a parchment-lined cookie sheet and bake 12–15 minutes until dry and firm to the touch. Turn the oven off and leave the biscuits in another 20–30 minutes. Remove them from oven, cool them on a baking rack, and store them in a cookie tin.

Pumpkin Pie Biscuits

These biscuits are perfect for Halloween and smell just like pumpkin pie.
Use a bat- or pumpkin-shaped cookie cutter for added fun.

1. Preheat the oven to 325°F.
2. Measure the flour, rolled oats, baking powder, cinnamon, and ginger into a mixing bowl. Whisk till combined.
3. Make a well in the flour and add the canola oil. Mix on medium speed using a paddle attachment till crumbly. Add the pumpkin and peanut butter, and stir till combined.
4. Add the water all at once and mix until dough forms and all the ingredients are combined.
5. Turn the dough out onto a slightly floured surface and gently knead until dough is smooth and soft. Roll the dough ¼-inch thick, and cut the biscuits into desired shapes with cookie cutters.
6. Place the biscuits on a parchment-lined cookie sheet and bake 12–15 minutes until they are dry and firm to the touch. Turn the oven off and leave the biscuits in another 20–30 minutes. Remove them from the oven, cool them on a baking rack, and store them in a cookie tin.

Yields 30 biscuits

1½ cups unbleached flour
1 cup rolled oats
2 teaspoons baking powder
1 teaspoon cinnamon
1 teaspoon ginger
2 tablespoons canola oil
½ cup pumpkin purée
¼ cup natural unsalted
    peanut butter
¼ cup filtered water

Canned Pumpkin
Considered a seasonal product, canned pumpkin is not always available year-round. Packed with vitamins and a flavor that dogs really enjoy, pumpkin is a healthy addition to dog biscuits. Buy several extra cans of pumpkin in the fall and keep them in your pantry for whenever you want to bake these biscuits. Use leftover pumpkin to bake the Pumpkin Spice Cake, page 184.

Sweet Potato Pie Biscuits

By combining the bacon and sweet potato, you create a biscuit that is both sweet and savory without the addition of unwanted sugar.

Yields 30 biscuits

1½ cups unbleached flour
1 cup rolled whole-wheat flour
2 teaspoons baking powder
1 teaspoon cinnamon
1 teaspoon ginger
2 tablespoons canola oil
½ cup cooked sweet potato, mashed
2 pieces Applegate Farms Sunday bacon, cooked and crumbled
¼ cup filtered water

Nitrates

Nitrates are used in curing meats to help prevent the growth of bacteria. Commonly found in bacon, cold cuts, dried sausages, and hot dogs, nitrates are not necessary. The body converts nitrates into carcinogens. Nitrate-free bacon is more expensive than the popular labels, but the taste and quality outweigh the cost.

1. Preheat the oven to 325ºF.
2. Measure the unbleached flour, whole-wheat flour, baking powder, cinnamon, and ginger into a mixing bowl. Whisk till combined.
3. Make a well in the flour and add the canola oil. Mix on medium speed using a paddle attachment till crumbly. Add the mashed sweet potato and bacon and stir until combined.
4. Add the water all at once and mix until dough forms and all the ingredients are combined.
5. Turn the dough out onto a slightly floured surface and gently knead until the dough is smooth and soft. Roll the dough ¼-inch thick, and cut the biscuits into desired shapes with cookie cutters.
6. Place the biscuits on a parchment-lined cookie sheet and bake 12–15 minutes till they are dry and firm to the touch. Turn the oven off and leave biscuits in another 20–30 minutes. Remove them from the oven, cool them on a baking rack, and store them in a cookie tin.

Winter Beef Barley Biscuits

Set a portion of the stew aside and add the mixture to kibble for a tasty dinner your dog will most certainly appreciate.

1. In a small skillet, heat the olive oil and sauté garlic over low heat. Add the chopped carrots and cook for about 5 minutes. Remove the carrots to cool.
2. Spread 2 tablespoons flour on a piece of waxed paper. Dredge the beef cubes in flour. Heat the skillet to medium high. Add the beef cubes to the skillet and cook. Remove from the heat and allow them to cool.
3. Pulse the cooked carrots, beef cubes, and garlic in a food processor until the mixture forms a paste. Set aside.
4. Preheat the oven to 325°F.
5. Whisk the flour, oats, and baking powder together in a mixing bowl. Make a well in the flour. Add the canola oil. Mix on medium speed using a paddle attachment until crumbly. Add the beef mixture and stir till combined. Add the beef broth all at once and mix till dough forms. Turn the dough out onto a slightly floured surface and gently knead. Roll the dough ¼-inch thick, and cut out the biscuits using a cookie cutter.
6. Place the biscuits on a parchment-lined cookie sheet and bake 12–15 minutes. Turn the oven off and leave the biscuits in another 20–30 minutes. Remove them from the oven, cool them on a baking rack, and store them in a cookie tin.

Yields 30 biscuits

1 tablespoon virgin olive oil
3 cloves garlic, finely chopped
2 carrots, peeled and chopped into chunks
2 tablespoons unbleached flour
¼ pound beef stew meat
1 cup unbleached flour
1 cup rolled oats
2 teaspoons baking powder
4 tablespoons canola oil
¼ cup natural beef broth

Bacon and Beet Biscuits

Ancient Romans enjoyed eating beets because they were considered an aid to digestion. Beets are the sweetest of all vegetables and can be served baked, boiled, roasted, or pickled.

Yields 30 biscuits

1 cup unbleached flour
1 cup rolled whole-wheat
    flour
2 teaspoons baking powder
2 tablespoons canola oil
1–2 cooked beets, finely diced
2 pieces Applegate Farms
    Sunday bacon, cooked
    and crumbled
¼ cup filtered water

Why Beets?

Dogs require fiber in their diets. It plays a vital role in intestinal health. The right kind of fiber maintains healthy bacteria in the colon and can even manage diarrhea. Dogs benefit the most from fiber sources that are moderately fermentable, such as beets. Beets contain vitamin C and are a good source of soluble and insoluble fiber as well as several antioxidants.

1. Preheat the oven to 325°F.
2. Measure the dry ingredients into a mixing bowl and whisk till combined.
3. Make a well in the flour, and add the canola oil. Mix on medium speed using a paddle attachment till crumbly. Add the diced beets and bacon, and stir until combined.
4. Add the water all at once, and mix until dough forms and all the ingredients are combined.
5. Turn the dough out onto a slightly floured surface and gently knead till dough is smooth and soft. Roll the dough ¼-inch thick and cut out the biscuits using a cookie cutter.
6. Place the biscuits on a parchment-lined cookie sheet and bake 12–15 minutes till they are dry and firm to the touch. Turn the oven off and leave the biscuits in another 20–30 minutes. Remove them from the oven, cool them on a baking rack, and store them in a cookie tin.

Savory Bacon, Cheddar, and Oatmeal Biscuits

These biscuits are so good that if you double the amount of cheese,
you can serve them at your next cocktail party and no one
would ever believe they are dog biscuits.

1. Preheat the oven to 325°F.
2. Measure the oats, flour, and baking powder into a mixing bowl and whisk until combined. Add the grated cheeses and bacon and stir until combined.
3. Make a well in the flour, and add the canola oil. Mix on medium speed using a paddle attachment till crumbly.
4. Add the water all at once, and mix till dough forms and all the ingredients are combined.
5. Turn the dough out onto a slightly floured surface and gently knead till dough is smooth and soft. Roll the dough ¼-inch thick, and cut out the biscuits using a cookie cutter.
6. Place the biscuits on a parchment-lined cookie sheet and bake 12–15 minutes till they are dry and firm to the touch. Turn the oven off and leave the biscuits in another 20–30 minutes. Remove them from the oven, cool them on a baking rack, and store them in a cookie tin.

Yields 30 biscuits

2 cups rolled oats
½ cup unbleached flour
2 teaspoons baking powder
½ cup natural Cheddar cheese, grated
1 tablespoon Romano cheese, freshly grated
2 pieces Applegate Farms Sunday bacon, cooked and crumbled
2 tablespoons canola oil
¼ cup filtered water

Peanut Butter and Bacon Oatmeal Biscuits

Remember this simple rule: Dough that is too sticky needs more flour, and dough that is too dry needs a little more water or canola oil.

Yields 30 biscuits

2 cups rolled oats
½ cup oat flour
2 teaspoons baking powder
2 pieces Applegate Farms Sunday bacon, cooked and crumbled
½ cup natural unsalted peanut butter
¼ cup filtered water

Sticky Situation

To keep biscuits from sticking, dip your cookie cutters in flour, tapping off the excess. Press straight down and try not to wiggle the cutter back and forth while trying to cut the dough. If the biscuit sticks to the cutter, simply poke it out directly onto the cookie sheet with your finger.

1. Preheat the oven to 325°F.
2. Measure the oats, flour, and baking powder into a mixing bowl and whisk till combined. Add the bacon and stir till combined.
3. Mix the peanut butter and water in a glass measuring cup. Make a well in the flour, and add the peanut butter and water mixture all at once. Mix on medium speed using a paddle attachment until combined. The mixture should form a soft dough.
4. Turn the dough out onto a lightly floured surface and gently knead till the dough is smooth and soft. Roll the dough ¼-inch thick, and cut out the biscuits using a cookie cutter.
5. Place the biscuits on a parchment-lined cookie sheet and bake for 12–15 minutes till they are dry and firm to the touch. Turn off the oven and leave the biscuits in another 20–30 minutes. Remove them from the oven, cool them on a baking rack, and store them in a cookie tin.

Carob, Peanut Butter, and Oatmeal Biscuits

Use a round fluted cookie cutter to shape these biscuits.

. . . .

1. Preheat the oven to 325°F.
2. Measure the dry ingredients into a mixing bowl and whisk till combined.
3. Mix the peanut butter, vanilla, and water in a glass measuring cup. Make a well in the flour, and add the peanut butter and water mixture all at once. On medium speed using a paddle attachment, mix until a soft dough forms.
4. Turn the dough out onto a slightly floured surface and gently knead till the dough is smooth and still soft. Roll the dough ¼-inch thick and cut out the biscuits using cookie cutters.
5. Place the biscuits on a parchment-lined cookie sheet and bake 12–15 minutes until they are dry and firm to the touch. Turn off the oven and leave the biscuits in another 20–30 minutes. Remove them from the oven, cool them on a baking rack, and store them in a cookie tin.

Yields 30 biscuits

2 cups rolled oats
½ cup oat flour
2 teaspoons baking powder
2 teaspoons cinnamon
2 tablespoons unsweetened carob powder
1 teaspoon pure vanilla
½ cup natural unsalted peanut butter
¼ cup filtered water

Sweet Topping
To make a shiny glaze for these biscuits combine equal parts of water and organic brown rice syrup and whisk until smooth. After the cookies have been baked and cooled, use a pastry brush to lightly brush the tops of the biscuits and place an unsweetened carob chip on top of each biscuit.

Chapter 4
Refrigerator Biscuits

Peanut Butter–Spice Biscuits

*If rice flour isn't available, you can substitute a combination
of rolled oats and oat flour. To make the oat flour, simply process rolled oats
in a food processor until it turns into a powder.*

Yields 30 biscuits

2 cups rice flour
½ cup rolled oats
2 teaspoons baking powder
1 teaspoon cinnamon
1 teaspoon ginger
½ cup natural peanut butter
¼ cup filtered water

Rice Flour

Whether you use brown or white rice flour, it can be tricky to work with. Its texture is almost sandy to the touch, and it forms a dough that crumbles easily. Although it can be frustrating to use, rice flour is recommended for dogs with wheat and corn allergies. If your dog can tolerate wheat flour, all the recipes in this section can be modified accordingly.

1. Preheat the oven to 325°F.
2. Measure the rice flour, rolled oats, baking powder, cinnamon, and ginger into a mixing bowl and whisk till combined.
3. Combine the peanut butter and water in glass measuring cup and stir with a fork till smooth and creamy.
4. Make a well in the flour, and pour in the peanut butter mixture. Mix on medium speed using a paddle attachment till just combined.
5. Turn the dough out onto a slightly floured surface and form into a log, about 2 inches in diameter. Wrap in plastic wrap and chill for 1 hour.
6. When ready to bake, slice the biscuits ⅛-inch thick and place on a parchment-lined cookie sheet. Bake 12–15 minutes till they are dry and firm to the touch. Turn the oven off and leave the biscuits in another 20–30 minutes. Remove them from the oven, cool them on a baking rack, and store them in a cookie tin.

Almond and Ginger Biscuits

If you don't have almonds available, try using almond butter. Similar to peanut butter, almond butter is widely available in natural and specialty markets.

1. Preheat the oven to 325°F.
2. Measure the rice flour, rolled oats, baking powder, ginger, crystallized ginger, and almonds into a mixing bowl, and whisk until combined. If you are using almond butter, do not add it at this stage.
3. Make a well in the flour, and add the canola oil. Mix on medium speed using a paddle attachment till crumbly.
4. Add the water all at once, and mix till dough forms and all the ingredients are combined. If you are using almond butter, combine it with the water in a glass measuring cup and stir with a fork till smooth and creamy. Add it to the flour and mix until combined.
5. Turn the dough out onto a slightly floured surface and form it into a log, about 2 inches in diameter. Wrap in plastic wrap and chill for 1 hour.
6. When ready to bake, slice the biscuits ⅛-inch thick and place them on a parchment-lined cookie sheet. Bake 12–15 minutes until they are dry and firm to the touch. Turn the oven off and leave the biscuits in another 20–30 minutes. Remove them from the oven, cool them on a baking rack, and store them in a cookie tin.

Yields 30 biscuits

2 cups rice flour
½ cup rolled oats
2 teaspoons baking powder
1 teaspoon ginger
2 teaspoons crystallized ginger
½ cup ground almonds
1 tablespoon canola oil
¼ cup filtered water

Sautéed Liver and Bacon Biscuits

*A little liver goes a long way, so store any uncooked liver in the freezer.
If you work with the liver when it is slightly frozen, it will
be easier to touch and reduce cleanup.*

Yields 30 biscuits

2 pieces Applegate Farms
    Sunday bacon
3 ounces calf or beef liver
2 cloves garlic
2 tablespoons canola oil or
    bacon drippings
¼ cup filtered water
2 cups rice flour
½ cup rolled oats
2 teaspoons baking powder

Sauté the French Way

The goal in sautéing food is to cook it in a small amount of fat in a shallow pan at high heat while preserving its color, moisture, and flavor. From the French verb *sauter*, which means "to jump," the food is meant to be flipped onto its other side by making it jump through the air.

1. Preheat the oven to 325°F.
2. Cook the bacon in a skillet until brown and crunchy. Allow to cool. Crumble by hand or pulse in the food processor.
3. Add the liver and garlic to the skillet with the bacon drippings and sauté till the liver is firm and no longer pink. Pulse the cooked liver in the food processor, and slowly add the canola oil or bacon drippings and process till the mixture forms a paste. Add water slowly and continue processing till smooth and creamy.
4. Measure the rice flour, rolled oats, and baking powder into a mixing bowl. Add the bacon crumbles and whisk till combined. Make a well in the flour, and add the liver mixture all at once. Mix on medium speed using a paddle attachment till dough forms and all the ingredients are combined.
5. Turn the dough out onto a slightly floured surface and form it into a log, about 2 inches in diameter. Wrap in plastic wrap and chill for 1 hour.
6. When ready to bake, slice the biscuits ⅛-inch thick and place them on a parchment-lined cookie sheet. Bake 12–15 minutes until they are dry and firm to the touch. Turn the oven off and leave the biscuits in another 20–30 minutes. Remove them from the oven, cool them on a baking rack, and store them in a cookie tin.

Fish and Chips Biscuits

For a change of pace, use canned salmon in place of the tuna. Canned salmon can contain bones, skin, and cartilage, so process the salmon in the food processor prior to using.

1. Preheat the oven to 325°F.
2. Measure the dry ingredients into a mixing bowl. Flake the tuna with a fork and add it to the flour mixture. Add the oil and mix till crumbly.
3. Make a well in the flour, and pour in the water all at once. Mix on medium speed using a paddle attachment until just combined.
4. Turn the dough out onto a slightly floured surface and form it into a log, about 2 inches in diameter. Wrap in plastic wrap and chill for 1 hour.
5. When ready to bake, slice the biscuits ⅛-inch thick, and place them on a parchment-lined cookie sheet. Bake 12–15 minutes till they are dry and firm to the touch. Turn the oven off and leave the biscuits in another 20–30 minutes. Remove them from oven, cool them on a baking rack and store them in a cookie tin.

Yields 30 biscuits

2 cups brown rice flour
½ cup rolled oats
2 teaspoons baking powder
3 ounces chunk light tuna packed in water
2 tablespoons canola oil
¼ cup filtered water

Swiss Cheese on Rye Biscuits

Any mild, hard cheese that can be grated will work in this recipe. Swiss cheese combines nicely with the rye flour and complements its intense flavor and smell.

Yields 30 biscuits

1 cup rolled oats
1 cup rye flour
2 teaspoons baking powder
½ cup Swiss cheese, grated
2 tablespoons canned
    crushed tomatoes
2 tablespoons canola oil
¼ cup filtered water

Purchasing Flour

Experimenting with various types of flour can be fun, but proceed cautiously. Purchase flours in small two-pound packages and be sure to check the expiration dates. Store in resealable plastic bags in the refrigerator and try to use within two months of opening.

1. Preheat the oven to 325°F.
2. Measure the rolled oats, rye flour, and baking powder into a mixing bowl and whisk till combined. Add the grated Swiss cheese and crushed tomatoes and stir until combined.
3. Make a well in the flour, and add the canola oil. Mix on medium speed using a paddle attachment until crumbly.
4. Add the water all at once, and mix until dough forms and all the ingredients are combined.
5. Turn the dough out onto a slightly floured surface and form it into a log, about 2 inches in diameter. Wrap in plastic wrap and chill for 1 hour.
6. When ready to bake, slice the biscuits ⅛-inch thick and place them on a parchment-lined cookie sheet. Bake 12–15 minutes until they are dry and firm to the touch. Turn the oven off and leave the biscuits in another 20–30 minutes. Remove them from the oven, cool them on a baking rack, and store them in a cookie tin.

Braised Beef and Carrot Biscuits

To save time, shred carrots and store in resealable plastic bags. The carrot can be used in biscuits or sprinkled over kibble for added color, crunch, and flavor.

1. In a small skillet, heat the olive oil and sauté garlic over low heat. Add the beef cubes to the skillet, break them apart with a fork, and cook them until browned. Remove them from the heat and allow to cool.
2. Preheat the oven to 325°F.
3. Measure the flour, rolled oats, and baking powder into a mixing bowl and whisk till combined. Add the carrot and cooked beef.
4. Make a well in the flour, and add the canola oil. Mix on medium speed using a paddle attachment until crumbly.
5. Add the beef broth all at once, and mix until dough forms. Turn the dough out onto a slightly floured surface and form it into a log, about 2 inches in diameter. Wrap in plastic wrap and chill for 1 hour.
6. When ready to bake, slice the biscuits ⅛-inch thick and place on a parchment-lined cookie sheet. Bake 12–15 minutes until dry and firm to the touch. Turn off the oven and leave the biscuits in the oven another 20–30 minutes. Remove them from the oven, cool them on a baking rack, and store them in a cookie tin.

Yields 30 biscuits

1 tablespoon virgin olive oil
2 cloves garlic
¼ pound beef stew meat, finely chopped
1 cup barley flour
1 cup rolled oats
2 teaspoons baking powder
1 carrot, peeled and shredded
4 tablespoons canola oil
¼ cup natural beef broth

Bleu Cheese and Tomato Biscuits

Bleu cheese can be purchased by the pound or crumbled in resealable containers from the deli or dairy section in your grocery. The intense smell and flavor really appeal to dogs.

Yields 30 biscuits

1 cup rolled oats
1 cup rice flour
2 teaspoons baking powder
½ cup natural bleu cheese, crumbled
2 tablespoons canned crushed tomatoes
2 tablespoons canola oil
¼ cup filtered water

Tomato Paste

Rather than opening a can of crushed tomatoes, you can easily infuse your recipes with a squeeze from a tube of tomato paste. Imparting an intense flavor and color, tomato paste is an easy shortcut and great substitution. When replacing crushed tomatoes with tomato paste, reduce the quantity called for in the recipe by half.

1. Preheat the oven to 325°F.
2. Measure the rolled oats, rice flour, and baking powder into a mixing bowl and whisk till combined. Add the crumbled bleu cheese and crushed tomatoes and stir till combined.
3. Make a well in the flour, and add the canola oil. Mix on medium speed using a paddle attachment until crumbly.
4. Add the water all at once, and mix until dough forms and all the ingredients are combined.
5. Turn the dough out onto a slightly floured surface and form it into a log, about 2 inches in diameter. Wrap in plastic wrap and chill for 1 hour.
6. When ready to bake, slice the biscuits ⅛-inch thick and place them on a parchment-lined cookie sheet. Bake 12–15 minutes until they are dry and firm to the touch. Turn off the oven and leave the biscuits in the oven another 20–30 minutes. Remove them from the oven, cool them on a baking rack, and store them in a cookie tin.

Savory Chicken and Vegetable Biscuits

Pecorino Romano is milder than Parmesan, and grating it as you need it insures freshness and flavor.

1. Heat a grill pan over medium heat. Toss the sliced chicken breast in the olive oil and place on the hot grill. Do not turn pieces until the chicken has grill marks and no longer sticks to the pan. If the chicken sticks, allow it to cook a minute longer.
2. Preheat the oven to 325°F.
3. Measure the dry ingredients into a mixing bowl and whisk till combined. Squeeze the excess water from the thawed broccoli. Add the broccoli and grated Romano cheese to the bowl.
4. Pour the chicken broth into the pan and scrape up the brown bits. Pour broth and canola oil into a glass measuring cup. Pulse the chicken in the food processor till coarsely chopped. Add the chicken to the broth mixture and stir.
5. Make a well in the flour and pour in the chicken mixture. Mix on medium speed using a paddle attachment until combined.
6. Turn the dough out onto a slightly floured surface and form it into a log, about 2 inches in diameter. Wrap in plastic wrap and chill for 1 hour.
7. Slice the biscuits ⅛-inch thick and place them on a parchment-lined cookie sheet. Bake 12–15 minutes. Turn oven off and leave biscuits in oven another 20–30 minutes. Remove them from the oven, cool them on a baking rack, and store them in a cookie tin.

Yields 30 biscuits

1 chicken breast, cut into thick slices
2 teaspoons virgin olive oil
1 cup barley flour
1 cup rolled oats
2 teaspoons baking powder
2 tablespoons frozen chopped broccoli, thawed
2 tablespoons freshly grated Romano cheese
½ cup organic free-range chicken broth
4 tablespoons canola oil

Sautéed Liver and Romano Cheese Biscuits

Rinse chicken livers, place in a resealable plastic bag, and put them in the freezer for two hours. Remove excess fat and any green bits with a sharp knife and chop before the liver thaws.

Yields 30 biscuits

3 ounces chicken livers, chopped
2 cloves garlic
2 tablespoons virgin olive oil
¼ cup filtered water
2 cups rice flour
½ cup rolled oats
2 teaspoons baking powder
2 tablespoons freshly grated Romano cheese

Fried Chicken Livers and Champagne

This treat is just for you. Combine equal parts of Romano cheese and bread crumbs. Season with freshly ground pepper. Dip bite-size pieces of cleaned chicken liver in a beaten egg. Coat liver pieces with the cheese-bread crumb mixture and sauté in virgin olive oil until browned. Serve with a glass of champagne and enjoy!

1. Preheat the oven to 325°F.
2. Sauté the chicken livers and garlic in the olive oil until the liver is firm and no longer pink. Pulse the cooked liver in a food processor. Slowly add the drippings and process the mixture until it forms a paste. Slowly add the water and continue processing till smooth and creamy.
3. Measure the rice flour, rolled oats, and baking powder into a mixing bowl. Add the grated cheese and whisk until combined. Make a well in the flour, and add the liver mixture all at once. Mix on medium speed using a paddle attachment until dough forms and all the ingredients are combined.
4. Turn the dough out onto a slightly floured surface and form into a log, about 2 inches in diameter. Wrap in plastic wrap and chill for 1 hour.
5. When ready to bake, slice the biscuits ⅛-inch thick and place them on a parchment-lined cookie sheet. Bake 12–15 minutes till they are dry and firm to the touch. Turn the oven off and leave the biscuits in another 20–30 minutes. Remove them from the oven, cool them on a baking rack, and store them in a cookie tin.

Dried Anchovy Biscuits

Dried anchovies have a very heady smell, so place the desired amount for this recipe in a resealable plastic bag and crush them into a powder with a rolling pin, can, or even your hands.

1. Preheat the oven to 325°F.
2. Measure the dry ingredients into a mixing bowl. Add the crumbled anchovies and flake with a fork. Add oil and mix till crumbly.
3. Combine the water and tomato paste in a glass measuring cup and stir until smooth. Make a well in the flour, and pour in the tomato water all at once. Mix on medium speed using a paddle attachment until just combined.
4. Turn the dough out onto a lightly floured surface and form it into a log, about 2 inches in diameter. Wrap in plastic wrap and chill for 1 hour.
5. When ready to bake, slice the biscuits ⅛-inch thick and place them on a parchment-lined cookie sheet. Bake 12–15 minutes until they are dry and firm to the touch. Turn the oven off and leave the biscuits in another 20–30 minutes. Remove them from the oven, cool them on a baking rack, and store them in a cookie tin.

Yields 30 biscuits

1 cup brown rice flour
2 cups rolled oats
2 teaspoons baking powder
¼ cup dried anchovies, crumbled
2 tablespoons canola oil
¼ cup filtered water
1 tablespoon tomato paste

Oatmeal, Date, and Cream Cheese Biscuits

Dates tend to be sticky. Dust them with some flour to make them easier to chop either by hand or in the food processor.

Yields 30 biscuits

2 cups rolled oats
½ cup rice flour
2 teaspoons baking powder
2 tablespoons chopped dates
4 ounces light cream cheese, softened
2 tablespoons canola oil
½ cup filtered water

Cream Cheese

Store cream cheese in the refrigerator tightly sealed in plastic wrap and a resealable plastic bag. Do not attempt to freeze cream cheese because it will break down while defrosting. To soften cream cheese quickly, place it in a microwave-safe dish and heat for 30 seconds at medium heat. A fork is the easiest and best tool for mashing and blending softened cream cheese.

1. Preheat the oven to 325°F.
2. Measure the rolled oats, rice flour, and baking powder into a mixing bowl and whisk till combined. Add the chopped dates and stir until combined.
3. In a separate bowl, beat the cream cheese and oil until blended. Make a well in the flour, and add the cream cheese and oil mixture. Mix on medium speed using a paddle attachment until crumbly.
4. Add the water all at once and mix until dough forms and all the ingredients are combined.
5. Turn the dough out onto a slightly floured surface and form it into a log, about 2 inches in diameter. Wrap in plastic wrap and chill for 1 hour.
6. When ready to bake, slice the biscuits ⅛-inch thick and place them on a parchment-lined cookie sheet. Bake 12–15 minutes till they are dry and firm to the touch. Turn the oven off and leave the biscuits in another 20–30 minutes. Remove them from the oven, cool them on a baking rack, and store them in a cookie tin.

Almond and Coconut Biscuits

The almonds and coconut can be prepared ahead of time.
Process the almonds and coconut together in a food processor. To toast,
place directly into a small skillet over high heat and stir constantly
or bake the mixture at 400ºF for 2–3 minutes.

1. Preheat the oven to 325ºF.
2. Measure the rice flour, rolled oats, baking powder, and ginger into a mixing bowl and whisk until combined. Add the toasted coconut and almonds.
3. Make a well in the flour and pour in the canola oil all at once. Mix on medium speed using a paddle attachment until just crumbly. Add the water all at once and mix until a soft dough forms.
4. Turn the dough out onto a lightly floured surface and form it into a log, about 2 inches in diameter. Wrap in plastic wrap and chill for 1 hour.
5. Slice the biscuits ⅛-inch thick and place them on a parchment-lined cookie sheet. Bake 12–15 minutes until they are dry and firm to the touch. Turn the oven off and leave the biscuits in another 20–30 minutes. Remove them from the oven, cool them on a baking rack, and store them in a cookie tin.

Yields 30 biscuits

2 cups rice flour
½ cup rolled oats
2 teaspoons baking powder
1 teaspoon ginger
¼ cup unsweetened coconut, chopped and toasted
½ cup almonds, finely chopped and toasted
2 tablespoons canola oil
¼ cup filtered water

Chapter 5

Decorated Biscuits

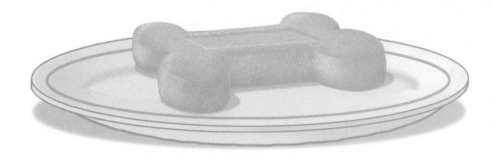

Birthday Bacon Crumbles

These no-bake treats can be made with any bacon, cheese, or peanut butter-flavored biscuit you have available. Keep the crumbles small and store them in the refrigerator until you are ready to serve them.

Yields 40 crumbles

¼ cup unsalted natural peanut butter
¼ cup cream cheese
¾ cup Peanut Butter, Carrot, and Wheat Germ Biscuits, page 34
4 pieces Applegate Farms Sunday bacon, cooked and crumbled

Easy Substitutions

You can always revise a recipe to suit your dog's palate or food intolerances. You can substitute unsweetened coconut for bacon. If you don't want to add cheese, use cooked rice. Try mashed sweet potato instead of peanut butter. Just make sure to add enough biscuit crumbles so the mixture will retain a shape.

1. Combine the peanut butter and cream cheese in a mixing bowl. Mix on medium speed using a paddle attachment until combined.
2. Place the biscuits in a plastic bag and gently crush them into small crumbles with a rolling pin. Add the bacon and broken biscuits to the peanut butter and cream cheese mixture, and mix until just combined.
3. Wet your hands and shape the mixture into small cubes or rounds. Store the crumbles in a sealed container in the refrigerator for up to one week.

Liver Pâté Napoleons

These party biscuits need to be assembled just prior to serving. Otherwise, the biscuits will become soggy, and the liver will form a dark crust.

1. Preheat the oven to 325°F.
2. Cook the bacon in a skillet till brown and crunchy. Allow it to cool. Crumble it by hand or pulse it in a food processor.
3. Add the liver and garlic to the bacon drippings, and sauté until firm and the liver is no longer pink. Pulse the cooked liver in a food processor and slowly add the beef broth. Process until the mixture forms a paste. Add the softened cream cheese and continue processing until smooth and creamy.
4. Measure the flour, rolled oats, and baking powder into a mixing bowl. Add two-thirds of the bacon crumbles and whisk until combined. Make a well in the flour, and add the canola oil. Using a paddle attachment, mix on medium speed until crumbly. Add the water all at once and mix till dough forms.
5. Turn the dough out onto a slightly floured surface and knead gently. Roll the dough ⅛-inch thick, and cut the dough into thirty 1 × 2-inch strips. Place the biscuits on a parchment-lined cookie sheet. Bake 12–15 minutes. Turn the oven off and leave the biscuits in another 20–30 minutes. Remove them from the oven and cool them on a baking rack.
6. When you are ready to serve the napoleons, spread a teaspoon of the liver and cream cheese mixture on each biscuit. Stack the biscuits in threes and sprinkle the top biscuit with additional bacon crumbles. Eat within two hours.

Yields 30 biscuits

3 pieces Applegate Farms Sunday bacon
3 ounces calf or beef liver
2 cloves garlic
2 tablespoons organic beef broth
2 tablespoons cream cheese, softened
1 cup unbleached flour
1 cup rolled oats
2 teaspoons baking powder
2 tablespoons canola oil
½ cup filtered water

Timing Tip

You can always bake the biscuits ahead of time, store them in a tin, and make the final preparations at the last minute. In a pinch, a coating of peanut butter will work just as well as cream cheese and liver.

New York–Style Pizza Biscuits

These biscuits smell so good when they are baking you'll swear you're in a pizza parlor! You can always eliminate the sausage and add other ingredients such as spinach or parsley if you prefer.

Yields 30 biscuits

2 teaspoons virgin olive oil
3 cloves garlic, chopped
¼ pound sweet Italian turkey sausage
1 cup unbleached flour
1 cup rolled oats
2 teaspoons baking powder
2 teaspoons garlic powder
½ cup mozzarella cheese, shredded
½ cup Italian "Gravy," page 198

Pizza Party

If you want to serve minipizzas at your dog's birthday party, try starting with a base of mini-whole-wheat pita breads. Warm them in the oven and top with tomato sauces and any toppings you desire. Bake pizzas in a 350-degree oven for 5–7 minutes. Be sure to make extra; these treats will be eaten by your two-legged guests as well as the four-legged ones!

1. Preheat the oven to 325°F.
2. In a small skillet, heat the olive oil and sauté the garlic over low heat. Remove the sausage casing and add the meat to the skillet. Using a wooden spoon, break the sausage apart into little "crumbles." Cook until the sausage bits are browned and nearly crunchy. Remove from the heat and allow to cool.
3. Measure the flour, rolled oats, baking powder, garlic powder, and mozzarella cheese into a mixing bowl and whisk till combined. Combine the cooked sausage bits, garlic, and oil into a glass measuring cup. Pour the Italian "Gravy" into the sausage mixture and stir with a fork until combined.
4. Make a well in the flour, and pour in the sausage mixture. Mix on medium speed using a paddle attachment till combined.
5. Turn the dough out onto a slightly floured surface and gently knead it till dough is smooth and still soft. Roll the dough ¼-inch thick, and cut the biscuits into desired shapes with cookie cutters.
6. Place the biscuits on a parchment-lined cookie sheet and bake 12–15 minutes until they are dry and firm to the touch. Turn the oven off and leave the biscuits in another 20–30 minutes. Remove them from the oven, cool them on a baking rack, and store them in a cookie tin.

Seven-Layer Biscuits

The beaten egg is the "glue" that holds the layers together.

1. Preheat the oven to 325°F.
2. Whisk the flour, baking powder, and cinnamon together into a mixing bowl, and whisk until combined. Divide the flour mixture in half. Add the carob powder to one-half of the mixture, and reserve it on a piece of waxed paper—this is the black layer. The other half is the white layer.
3. Combine the peanut butter and water in glass measuring cup, and stir until smooth and creamy. Make a well in the white layer and pour in half of the peanut butter mixture. Mix on medium speed. Remove the dough and cover it with a damp paper towel.
4. Add the black layer to the bowl and pour in the remaining peanut butter mixture. Mix on medium speed.
5. Turn each lump of dough onto a slightly floured surface and shape them into flat discs. Flatten each disc to ¼-inch thickness. Apply a thin coating of the beaten egg to the top of the black layer. Carefully lift the white layer and place it on top of the black layer, pressing them together. Chill in the freezer for 10 minutes.
6. Cut the dough in half lengthwise. Spread more egg on the white layer of one of the halves. Place the other half on top. Return the dough to the freezer for another 10 minutes. Slice the layers lengthwise into three even strips. Divide each strip into ¼-inch slices.
7. Bake 12–15 minutes. Turn the oven off and leave the biscuits in another 20–30 minutes.

Yields 30 biscuits

2 cups pastry flour
2 teaspoons baking powder
2 teaspoons cinnamon
1 tablespoon unsweetened carob powder
½ cup natural unsalted peanut butter
¼ cup filtered water
1 organic egg, beaten with 1 teaspoon water

Cheesy Linzer Tarts

Linzer tarts are not really tarts. They are a sandwich of two cookies—in this case, biscuits that have a layer of filling between them. A small cut-out from the top layer is a "window" to the filling.

Yields 15 sandwiches

2 cups pastry flour
2 teaspoons garlic powder
2 tablespoons Romano
    cheese, grated
2 tablespoons canola oil
¼ cup filtered water
2 tablespoons goat cheese,
    room temperature
1 tablespoon crushed
    tomatoes

Goat Cheese

Goat cheese is made from goat's milk and has a sharp and tangy taste. There are many varieties available because the cheese's consistency and flavor marries well with herbs, fruits, and even nuts. When goat cheese is marinated in virgin olive oil, it seals in the flavor and can keep for several months. Goat cheese can also be frozen without loss of texture or consistency.

1. Preheat the oven to 325°F.
2. Measure the flour, garlic powder, and Romano cheese into a mixing bowl and whisk till combined.
3. Make a well in the flour and pour in the canola oil all at once. Mix on medium speed using a paddle attachment until crumbly. Add the water and continue mixing until a soft dough forms.
4. Turn the dough out onto a slightly floured surface and gently knead till dough is smooth and still soft. Roll the dough ¼-inch thick and cut an even number of 1-inch biscuits. Using a mini–cookie cutter, cut a window in half of the biscuits. Leftover bits of dough can be formed into another biscuit.
5. Place the biscuits on a parchment-lined cookie sheet and bake 12–15 minutes till they are dry and firm to the touch. Turn the oven off and leave the biscuits in another 20–30 minutes. Remove them from the oven, cool them on a baking rack, and store them in a cookie tin till ready to fill.
6. Use a fork to combine the softened goat cheese with the crushed tomatoes. Spread a thin layer of the cheese mixture on a plain biscuit and top with a biscuit that has a window. Repeat until the biscuit sandwiches are filled.

Bacon Snickerdoodles

Since these biscuits are topped with bacon crumbles, they are truly a treat and should be doled out in moderation. You can also try substituting turkey bacon, but it never crisps the same way pork bacon does. Try processing the turkey bacon in a food processor and crisp it further by pan-frying it a second time.

1. Preheat the oven to 325°F.
2. Measure the unbleached flour, whole-wheat flour, and baking powder into a mixing bowl and whisk till combined.
3. Combine the peanut butter, carrot, and water in a glass measuring cup and stir with a fork until smooth and creamy.
4. Make a well in the flour and pour in the peanut butter mixture. Mix on medium speed using a paddle attachment until combined.
5. Turn the dough out onto a slightly floured surface and gently knead it till dough is smooth and still soft. Roll the dough ¼-inch thick and cut the biscuits into 1-inch diameter circles, using a fluted cookie cutter.
6. Place the biscuits on a parchment-lined cookie sheet and brush with some of the beaten egg. While the biscuits are still wet, sprinkle with the crumbled bacon. Use a glass or your fingers to press the bacon on the biscuits. Bake 12–15 minutes until dry and firm to the touch. Turn off the oven and leave the biscuits in oven another 20–30 minutes. Remove them from the oven, cool them on a baking rack, and store them in a cookie tin.

Yields 30 biscuits

1 cup unbleached flour
1 cup whole-wheat flour
2 teaspoons baking powder
½ cup unsalted natural peanut butter
2 tablespoons carrot, grated
½ cup filtered water
1 organic egg, beaten
2 pieces Applegate Farms Sunday bacon, cooked and crumbled

Fluted Cookie Cutters

Sets of fluted cookie cutters are available in round, oval, and square shapes. They come packed in a tin that contains sets of five to eleven pieces, or you can purchase them individually. The graduated sizes are perfect for cutting the biscuits in the size you want for your size dog.

Coconut Granola Bars

Brown rice syrup is a sweetener made by culturing brown rice with enzymes and cooking it until the starches break down and the desired consistency is achieved. Rice syrup has a shelf life of about a year; once opened, it should be stored in a cool, dry place.

Yields 30 bars

2½ cups old-fashioned rolled oats
½ cup unsweetened flaked coconut
1 teaspoon cinnamon
2 teaspoons flaxseed, if desired
½ cup natural unsalted crunchy peanut butter
½ cup organic brown rice syrup

Woodstock

Believe it or not, we have the hippies who attended the 1969 Woodstock Music and Art Festival to thank for granola. Consisting of oats, nuts, dates, and dried fruit, the snack became popular because it was lightweight and provided a good source of energy. It was also relatively inexpensive and easy to store.

1. Preheat the oven to 350°F.
2. Combine the oats, coconut, cinnamon, and flaxseed in a mixing bowl and whisk until combined.
3. Combine the peanut butter and brown rice syrup in a glass measuring cup and stir with a fork until smooth and creamy.
4. Mix the oats and the peanut butter mixture on medium speed using a paddle attachment until combined. The mixture will be sticky.
5. Using a piece of parchment paper, press the oat mixture onto a parchment-lined jelly roll pan. Bake 12–15 minutes until golden and crispy. Allow to cool and use a knife to cut into small bars.

Sweet Pea Tarts

In this recipe, peas and potatoes replace the berries and custard you would normally see in a traditional fruit tart.

. . . .

1. Preheat the oven to 350°F. Defrost the phyllo shells, place them on a cookie sheet, and bake them for 5 minutes or until crisp.
2. While the baked potatoes are still warm, use a fork and mash them with the chicken broth and grated cheese. Fill the tart shells with warmed mashed-potato mixture, trying to round the top of the filling. Gently press the peas onto the potato filling, covering completely as if it were a fruit tart. Serve immediately.

Yields 15 minitarts

1 box mini–phyllo dough
   shells
2 potatoes, baked
2 tablespoons organic
   chicken broth
2 tablespoons freshly grated
   Romano cheese
½ cup frozen peas, thawed

Fillo or Phyllo

Fillo is a paper-thin sheet of dough that is easily layered, formed, and baked. The dough can be used to create everything from sweet to savory dishes and is known for its delightful crunch and flakiness. Phyllo dough is most famous for its use in the Greek dessert baklava, a honey and nut pastry, and spanikopita, a turn-over filled with spinach and feta cheese.

Sweet Potato Oven Chips

You can use any type of potato you prefer, but the sweet potato's natural sweetness combines with the cheese to create a perfect blend of sweet and savory. If you want to offer the chips to your family, simply sprinkle their portion with a little sea salt or kosher salt.

Yield 1 cup

1 sweet potato
¼ cup virgin olive oil
1 tablespoon freshly grated
    Romano cheese

The First Chip

Ironically, the potato chip, that beloved American snack, was born out of anger. One persnickety customer at Moon's Lake House near Saratoga Springs, New York, kept sending his fried potatoes back to the kitchen, complaining they weren't crisp enough. Chef George Crum made the potatoes as crisp as he could. To Crum's chagrin, the guest was thrilled. They became an immediate hit, and the lodge included what it dubbed "Saratoga Chips" on its regular menu.

1. Preheat the oven to 350°F.
2. Wash and peel the sweet potato. Slice it crosswise into very thin slices and place it in a single layer on a parchment-lined cookie sheet.
3. Using a silicon pastry brush, lightly coat the potato slices with the olive oil. Place them in the oven and bake for 30 minutes or until the potato slices are crisp and crunchy.
4. Remove the cookie sheet and sprinkle the "chips" with the grated cheese. Return the pan to the oven and allow the cheese to set for a minute or two. Cool the chips and store them in a resealable plastic bag at room temperature. Eat within three days.

Roasted Beet Chips

Peeling beets can be a bit tedious. A vegetable peeler will work with some effort, but you can always use a sharp paring knife if you prefer.

1. Preheat the oven to 350°F.
2. Wash and peel the beets. Slice them cross-wise into very thin slices and place them in a single layer on a parchment-lined cookie sheet.
3. Using a silicon pastry brush, lightly coat the beet slices with the olive oil. Place them in the oven and bake for 30 minutes or until the beet slices are crisp and crunchy.
4. Cool the chips and store them in a resealable plastic bag at room temperature. Eat within three days.

Yield 1 cup

3 red beets
¼ cup virgin olive oil

Bag of Chips

Once potato chips became popular, local markets piled them in barrels or tins. The chips at the bottom were often stale and damp. Laura Scudder, a California entrepreneur, was the first to package potato chips in bags. She came up with the idea of ironing two pieces of waxed paper together to create a bag with an airtight seal, thus keeping the chips fresh until opened. Her company was also the first company to add freshness dates to her product packaging.

Peanut Butter–Berry Buttons

If you are fortunate enough to travel to Maine during the summer, their wild blueberries are the perfect size for these biscuits. The berries are small, tart, and full of wonderful flavor.

Yields 30 biscuits

1 cup unbleached flour
½ cup whole-wheat flour
2 teaspoons baking powder
2 teaspoons cinnamon
½ cup natural unsalted
    peanut butter
¼ cup blueberries, chopped
½ cup filtered water

Blueberry Power

Blueberries are packed with a number of nutrients like vitamin C, manganese, vitamin E, and only a few calories. Blueberries also contain antioxidants called anthocyanidins and help neutralize the matrix of cells and tissues that potentially lead to heart disease, peptic ulcers, cataracts, and glaucoma. They also protect the brain against age-related conditions such as dementia and Alzheimer's disease.

1. Preheat the oven to 325°F.
2. Measure the unbleached flour, whole-wheat flour, baking powder, and cinnamon into a mixing bowl and whisk till combined.
3. Combine the peanut butter, blueberries, and water in a glass measuring cup, and stir with a fork until smooth and creamy.
4. Make a well in the flour and pour in the peanut butter mixture. Mix on medium speed using a paddle attachment until combined.
5. Turn the dough out onto a slightly floured surface and gently knead it till dough is smooth and still soft. Roll the dough ¼-inch thick and cut the biscuits into 1-inch round biscuits. Using a two-pronged fork or a skewer, poke each biscuit with "buttonholes."
6. Place the biscuits on a parchment-lined cookie sheet and bake 12–15 minutes until they are dry and firm to the touch. Turn the oven off and leave the biscuits in another 20–30 minutes. Remove them from the oven, cool them on a baking rack, and store them in a cookie tin.

Chapter 6

Biscotti

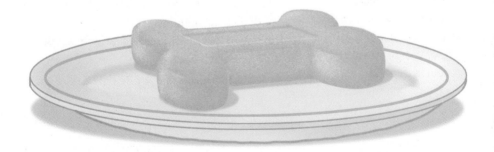

Green Apple Pie and Cheddar Biscotti

If you don't have pastry flour, any unbleached flour will work. Pastry flour is lighter, is easy to work with, and results in flakier biscotti.

- -

Yields 100 crouton-size biscuits

2 cups pastry flour or unbleached flour
2 teaspoon baking powder
½ green apple, coarsely chopped
¼ cup natural Cheddar cheese, grated
2 tablespoons canola oil
¼ cup filtered water

Biscotti

Biscotti are crisp Italian cookies that are baked twice. Traditionally, biscotti are formed into two long slabs, baked for 25 minutes, cut into ½-inch wedges, and returned to the oven to dry and crisp. The method described in the recipes in this chapter was developed for the ease of preparation and to create biscotti that are a dog-friendly shape.

1. Preheat the oven to 325°F.
2. Measure the flour, baking powder, apple, and cheese into a mixing bowl. Whisk until combined.
3. Make a well in the flour and pour in the canola oil. Combine with an electric mixer on medium speed using a paddle attachment. Mix until crumbly.
4. Add the water all at once and mix until it is just combined. The mixture should form a soft dough.
5. Turn the dough out onto a slightly floured surface and shape into a flat disc. Place the disc on a parchment-lined cookie sheet. Use a rolling pin to flatten the dough to ½-inch thickness.
6. Bake 18–25 minutes till it is dry and firm to the touch. Remove the dough from the oven and cool slightly. Using either a knife or pizza cutter, cut the dough into ½-inch strips. Rotate the pan and cut the strips into ½-inch cubes. Separate the cubes and return the pan to the oven; bake the biscuits another 15–20 minutes. Remove the biscotti from oven, cool them on a baking rack, and store them in a cookie tin.

Peanut Butter and Bacon Biscotti

A pizza cutter is the perfect tool for cutting the biscotti into crouton-shaped, bite-size bits. If you don't have a pizza cutter handy, a serrated knife will also work.

. . . .

1. Preheat the oven to 325°F.
2. Measure the flour, baking powder, and bacon into a mixing bowl and whisk till combined.
3. Combine the peanut butter and water in a glass measuring cup and stir with a fork until the mixture is smooth and creamy.
4. Make a well in the flour and pour in the peanut butter mixture. Combine with an electric mixer on medium speed using a paddle attachment. Mix till just combined.
5. Turn the dough out onto a slightly floured surface and shape into a flat disc. Place the disc on a parchment-lined cookie sheet. Use a rolling pin to flatten the dough to a ½-inch thickness.
6. Bake 18–25 minutes until it is dry and firm to the touch. Remove the dough from the oven, cool it slightly and cut it into ½-inch strips using either a knife or pizza cutter. Rotate the pan and cut the strips into ½-inch cubes. Separate the cubes and return the pan to the oven; bake the biscotti another 15–20 minutes. Remove them from the oven, cool them on a baking rack, and store them in a cookie tin.

Yields 100 crouton-size biscuits

2 cups pastry flour or unbleached flour
2 teaspoons baking powder
2 pieces bacon, preferably Applegate Farms Sunday bacon, cooked and crumbled
½ cup natural peanut butter
¼ cup filtered water

Hardy Bites

Biscotti can be stored for long periods. Explorers and soldiers have enjoyed biscotti for generations, and now your dog can, too!

Cranberry Coconut Biscotti

When buying dried fruit, read the ingredients and avoid purchasing products preserved with sulfites and added sugar.

Yields 100 crouton-size biscuits

2 cups pastry flour or unbleached flour
2 teaspoons baking powder
¼ cup dried cranberries, chopped
¼ cup unsweetened shredded coconut
2 tablespoons canola oil
¼ cup filtered water

Sulfites

Most often found in processed foods, sulfites are inorganic salts. They are used to prevent the oxidation or "browning" of light-colored fruits and vegetables such as apples and precut potatoes. Sulfites can cause allergic reactions in some individuals, including hives, facial swelling and tightness, and even difficulty breathing.

1. Preheat the oven to 325°F.
2. Measure the flour, baking powder, cranberries, and coconut into a mixing bowl. Whisk till combined.
3. Make a well in the flour and pour in the canola oil. Combine with an electric mixer on medium speed using a paddle attachment. Mix until crumbly.
4. Add the water all at once and mix till just combined. The mixture should form a soft dough.
5. Turn the dough out onto a slightly floured surface and shape it into a flat disc. Place the disc on a parchment-lined cookie sheet. Use a rolling pin to flatten the dough to a ½-inch thickness.
6. Bake 18–25 minutes until it is dry and firm to the touch. Remove the dough from the oven and cool it slightly. Cut it into ½-inch strips using either a pizza cutter or a knife. Rotate the pan and cut the strips into ½-inch cubes. Separate the cubes and return the pan to the oven. Bake the biscuits another 15–20 minutes. Remove the biscotti from the oven, cool them on a baking rack, and store them in a cookie tin.

Roasted Tomato and Mozzarella Biscotti

There are several brands of fire-roasted crushed tomatoes available at your local grocery store. The flavor is smoky, rich, and intense.

1. Preheat the oven to 325°F.
2. Measure the flour, baking powder, tomatoes, and mozzarella into a mixing bowl. Whisk till combined.
3. Make a well in the flour and pour in the canola oil. Combine with an electric mixer on medium speed using a paddle attachment. Mix until crumbly.
4. Add the water all at once and mix until just combined. The mixture should form a soft dough.
5. Turn the dough out onto a slightly floured surface and shape it into a flat disc. Place the disc on a parchment-lined cookie sheet and use a rolling pin to flatten the dough to a ½-inch thickness.
6. Bake 18–25 minutes till it is dry and firm to the touch. Remove the dough from the oven and cool slightly. Cut it into ½-inch strips using either a knife or pizza cutter. Rotate the pan and cut the strips into ½-inch cubes. Separate the cubes and return the pan to the oven. Bake the biscuits another 15–20 minutes. Remove the biscotti from the oven, cool them on a baking rack, and store them in a cookie tin.

Yields 100 crouton-size biscuits

2 cups pastry flour or unbleached flour
2 teaspoons baking powder
2 tablespoons canned fire-roasted crushed tomatoes
¼ cup natural mozzarella, shredded
2 tablespoons canola oil
¼ cup filtered water

Peanut Butter and Carob Chip Biscotti

Available in health-food stores, carob is the chocolate substitute that is appropiate for dogs. Store opened bags in a clearly labeled resealable bag.

Yields 100 crouton-size biscuits

2 cups pastry flour or
    unbleached flour
2 teaspoons baking powder
2 tablespoons unsweetened
    carob chips
½ cup natural unsalted
    peanut butter
¼ cup filtered water

Carob

Similar in taste to sweetened cocoa, carob does not contain caffeine or other elements that can affect the nervous system. Chocolate is toxic to dogs, and carob is a very popular substitution when creating bakery-style dog treats. Whether purchasing carob chips or powder, be sure to use only unsweetened varieties.

1. Preheat oven to 325°F.
2. Measure the flour, baking powder, and carob chips into a mixing bowl. Whisk till combined.
3. Combine peanut butter and water in a glass measuring cup and stir with a fork till smooth and creamy.
4. Make a well in the flour and pour in the peanut butter mixture. Combine with an electric mixer on medium speed using a paddle attachment. Mix until just combined.
5. Turn the dough out onto a slightly floured surface and shape it into a flat disc. Place the disc on a parchment-lined cookie sheet and use a rolling pin to flatten the dough to a ½-inch thickness.
6. Bake 18–25 minutes until it is dry and firm to the touch. Remove the dough from the oven, cool slightly, and cut it into ½-inch strips with either a knife or pizza cutter. Rotate the pan and cut the strips into ½-inch cubes. Separate the cubes and return the pan to the oven; bake the biscuits another 15–20 minutes. Remove the biscotti from the oven, cool them on a baking rack, and store them in a cookie tin.

Sautéed Liver and Bacon Biscotti

Cook a whole package of bacon, allow the slices to cool, and crumble them into bits. Store them in the freezer in a sealable plastic bag, and you will have your own bacon bits always at the ready.

1. Preheat the oven to 325°F.
2. Cook the bacon in a skillet until brown and crunchy. Allow the bacon to cool. Crumble it by hand or pulse it in a food processor.
3. Add the liver to the skillet with the bacon drippings. Add the garlic and sauté until the liver is firm and no longer pink. Pulse the cooked liver and the garlic cloves in a food processor and slowly add the canola oil or bacon drippings. Process till the mixture forms a paste. Add the water slowly, and continue processing till smooth and creamy.
4. Whisk the flour, baking powder, and bacon bits together.
5. Make a well in the flour and add the liver mixture all at once. Combine with an electric mixer on medium speed using a paddle attachment. Mix till dough forms and all the ingredients are thoroughly combined.
6. Turn the dough out onto a slightly floured surface and shape it into a flat disc. Flatten the dough to a ½-inch thickness.
7. Bake 18–25 minutes. Remove the dough from the oven, cool it slightly, and cut it into ½-inch strips. Rotate the pan and cut the strips into ½-inch cubes. Separate the cubes and return pan to oven. Bake biscuits for another 15–20 minutes. Remove the biscotti from the oven, cool them on a baking rack, and store them in a cookie tin.

Yields 100 crouton-size biscuits

2 pieces bacon, preferably Applegate Farms Sunday bacon
3 ounces calf or beef liver
2 cloves garlic
2 tablespoons canola oil or bacon drippings
¼ cup filtered water
2 cups pastry flour or unbleached flour
2 teaspoons baking powder

Carob and Almond Biscotti

You can substitute peanut butter for the almond butter. Either way, make sure you are buying and using nut butters that are unsweetened and unsalted.

Yields 100 crouton-size biscuits

2 cups pastry flour or unbleached flour
2 teaspoons baking powder
1 tablespoon unsweetened carob powder
¼ cup almonds, finely chopped
2 tablespoons natural unsalted almond butter
¼ cup filtered water

Walking Treats

Bite-size biscotti are the perfect treats to take with you. You can pack them in small snack containers and keep them in your car, back-pack, or purse. Save a small water bottle and keep it filled with fresh water. Your dog will be happy, and he won't even mind if the water is warm.

1. Preheat the oven to 325°F.
2. Measure the flour, baking powder, carob powder, and almonds into a mixing bowl. Whisk till combined.
3. Combine the almond butter and water in a glass measuring cup and stir with a fork until the mixture is smooth and creamy.
4. Make a well in the flour and pour in the almond butter mixture. Combine with an electric mixer on medium speed using a paddle attachment. Mix till just combined.
5. Turn the dough out onto a slightly floured surface and shape it into a flat disc. Place the disc on a parchment-lined cookie sheet and use a rolling pin to flatten the dough to a ½-inch thickness.
6. Bake 18–25 minutes till it is dry and firm to the touch. Remove from the oven, cool slightly, and cut into ½-inch strips with either a knife or pizza cutter. Rotate the pan and cut the strips into ½-inch cubes. Separate the cubes and return the pan to the oven. Bake the biscuits another 15–20 minutes. Remove the biscotti from the oven, cool them on a baking rack, and store them in a cookie tin.

Peas and Carrot Biscotti

For added flavor, try sautéing the peas and carrots in virgin olive oil and garlic before adding them to the dry ingredients.

- -

1. Preheat the oven to 325°F.
2. Measure the flour, baking powder, peas, and carrots into a mixing bowl. Whisk till combined.
3. Make a well in the flour and add the canola oil. Combine with an electric mixer on medium speed using a paddle attachment. Mix until crumbly.
4. Add the water all at once and mix until just combined. The mixture should form a soft dough.
5. Turn the dough out onto a slightly floured surface and shape it into a flat disc. Place the disc on a parchment-lined cookie sheet and use a rolling pin to flatten the dough to a ½-inch thickness.
6. Bake 18–25 minutes until it is dry and firm to the touch. Remove from the oven, cool slightly, and cut into ½-inch strips using either a knife or pizza cutter. Rotate the pan and cut the strips into ½-inch cubes. Separate the cubes and return the pan to the oven. Bake the biscuits another 15–20 minutes. Remove the biscotti from the oven, cool them on a baking rack, and store them in a cookie tin.

Yields 100 crouton-size biscuits

2 cups pastry flour or unbleached flour
2 teaspoons baking powder
¼ cup frozen peas and carrots, defrosted
2 tablespoons canola oil
¼ cup filtered water

Carob and Cherry Biscotti

*Available in health-food stores, carob powder is an alternative to
cocoa powder that is friendly to your dog. If the carob powder clumps,
pass it through a sifter before adding it to the dry ingredients.*

Yields 100 crouton-size biscuits

2 cups pastry flour or
   unbleached flour
2 teaspoons baking powder
1 tablespoon unsweetened
   carob powder
¼ cup dried cherries, chopped
2 tablespoons natural
   unsalted peanut butter
¼ cup filtered water

1. Preheat the oven to 325°F.
2. Measure the flour, baking powder, carob powder, and cherries into a mixing bowl and whisk till combined.
3. Combine the peanut butter and water in a glass measuring cup and stir with a fork until the mixture is smooth and creamy.
4. Make a well in the flour and pour in the peanut butter mixture. Combine with an electric mixer on medium speed using a paddle attachment. Mix till just combined.
5. Turn the dough out onto a slightly floured surface and shape it into a flat disc. Place the disc on a parchment-lined cookie sheet and use a rolling pin to flatten the dough to a ½-inch thickness.
6. Bake 18–25 minutes until it is dry and firm to the touch. Remove it from the oven, cool slightly, and cut it into ½-inch strips using either a knife or pizza cutter. Rotate the pan and cut the strips into ½-inch cubes. Separate the cubes and return the pan to the oven. Bake the biscuits another 15–20 minutes. Remove the biscotti from the oven, cool them on a baking rack, and store them in a cookie tin.

Time-Saving Tip

Premeasure dry ingredients and cut up nuts and dried fruits ahead of time. Store ingredients together in a bag. Using a permanent marker, label each bag with the name of the recipe, the name of the cookbook, and the page number, and store the bag in the refrigerator up to one month. When you're ready to bake, simply pour the mixed ingredients into the mixing bowl and add the wet ingredients.

BBQ Beef Biscotti

Organic and natural meat and vegetable broths are now available in coated resealable cartons. The broth will keep for a week in the refrigerator, and unused broth can be frozen in ice-cube trays and kept in resealable plastic bags.

* *

1. Preheat the oven to 325°F.
2. In a small skillet, heat the olive oil and sauté the garlic over low heat. Add the beef to the skillet and cook till the meat is well browned on all sides. Remove it from the pan and toss it with the barbecue sauce. Chop the stew meat into small bits and set aside.
3. Measure the beef, flour, and baking powder into a mixing bowl. Whisk till combined.
4. Make a well in the flour and add the canola oil. Combine with an electric mixer on medium speed using a paddle attachment. Mix till crumbly. Add the beef broth all at once and mix till just combined. The mixture should form a soft dough.
5. Turn the dough out onto a slightly floured surface and shape it into a flat disc. Place the disc on a parchment-lined cookie sheet and use a rolling pin to flatten the dough to a ½-inch thickness.
6. Bake 18–25 minutes until it is dry and firm to the touch. Remove it from the oven, cool slightly, and cut it into ½-inch strips using either a knife or pizza cutter. Rotate the pan and cut the strips into ½-inch cubes. Separate the cubes and return the pan to the oven. Bake the biscuits another 15–20 minutes. Remove the biscotti from the oven, cool them on a baking rack, and store them in a cookie tin.

Yields 100 crouton-size biscuits

1 tablespoon virgin olive oil
3 cloves garlic, minced
¼ pound beef stew meat
2 tablespoons prepared
    barbecue sauce
2 cups pastry flour
2 teaspoons baking powder
4 tablespoons canola oil
¼ cup natural beef broth

Blueberry Almond Biscotti

The blueberry-infused biscuit dough will turn a light purple and darken a bit as it bakes.

Yields 100 crouton-size biscuits

2 cups pastry flour
2 teaspoons baking powder
1 teaspoon cinnamon
¼ cup dried blueberries, chopped
¼ cup almonds, finely chopped
2 tablespoons natural unsalted almond butter
¼ cup filtered water

Rehydrating Blueberries

If you boil water and pour it over the dried blueberries, they will plump nicely. To chop, run the plumped berries and the berry water through the food processor until it turns to soup.

1. Preheat the oven to 325°F.
2. Measure the dry ingredients including blueberries and chopped almonds into a mixing bowl and whisk until combined.
3. Combine the almond butter and water in a glass measuring cup and stir with a fork until smooth and creamy.
4. Make a well in the flour and pour in the almond butter mixture. On medium speed using a paddle attachment, mix until just combined.
5. Turn the dough out onto a slightly floured surface and form them into a flat disc. Place the disc on a parchment-lined cookie sheet; using a rolling pin, flatten the dough to a ½-inch thickness.
6. Bake it 18–25 minutes until dry and firm to the touch. Remove from the oven, and cool slightly. Using either a knife or pizza cutter, cut it into ½-inch strips. Turn the pan and cut strips into ½-inch cubes. Separate the cubes, and return the pan to the oven; bake the biscuits another 15–20 minutes. Remove the biscotti from oven, cool them on baking rack, and store them in cookie tin.

Cheddar and Tomato Biscotti

The rye flour combined with the tomato paste will create a dark dough.

1. Preheat the oven to 325°F.
2. Measure the flours, baking powder, and cheese into a mixing bowl and whisk until combined.
3. Combine the tomato paste and water in a glass measuring cup and stir with a fork till smooth.
4. Make a well in the flour and pour in the tomato mixture all at once. Mix on medium speed using a paddle attachment until just combined.
5. Turn the dough out onto a lightly floured surface and form it into a flat disc. Place the disc on a parchment-lined cookie sheet, and using a rolling pin, flatten the dough to a ½-inch thickness.
6. Bake 18–25 minutes until it is dry and firm to the touch. Remove it from the oven, cool slightly, and use either a knife or pizza cutter to cut the dough into ½-inch strips. Turn the pan and cut the strips into ½-inch cubes. Separate the cubes, return the pan to the oven, and bake the biscuits another 15–20 minutes. Remove the biscotti from oven, cool on a baking rack, and store in a cookie tin.

Yields 100 crouton-size biscuits

1 cup pastry flour
1 cup rye flour
2 teaspoons baking powder
½ cup natural sharp Cheddar cheese, grated
2 tablespoons tomato paste
¼ cup filtered water

Tomato Tips

If you prefer, you can use canned chopped tomatoes that have been patted dry and shredded into small bits instead of tomato paste. Dust the bits lightly with flour before adding them to the flour mixture.

Chapter 7
Training Treats

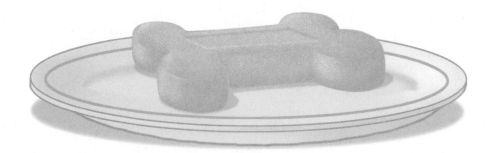

Bleu Cheese Pop 'Ems

*Rolling the pop 'ems is a perfect job for a preschooler,
and the results are nearly immediate.*

Yields 1 cup

¾ cup plain shredded wheat
   cereal
¼ cup natural bleu cheese,
   crumbled
2 ounces cream cheese, room
   temperature

Getting Kids Involved

It is never too early to teach your children about nutrition, whether it's their own or the family dog's. If they learn that Fifi should eat only food that has been bought or prepared for her, they won't be tempted to slip her scraps from the table or offer her any other "people food."

1. Place the cereal in a plastic bag and use a rolling pin to crush it into crumbs.
2. Place the bleu cheese and cream cheese on a plate, and mash them with a fork until they are smooth and combined.
3. Pour the crumbs into a bowl, and add the bleu cheese–cream cheese mixture. Mix until combined but still soft.
4. Roll the mixture into small balls, about the size of a gumball.
5. Store them in a resealable plastic bag in the refrigerator for up to one week.

Turkey Sausage Crumbles

These "crumbles" are addictive! Offer them sparingly and be sure to bring a bottle of water with you if you're training outside.

1. Preheat the oven to 325°F.
2. In a small skillet, heat the olive oil and sauté the garlic over low heat. Remove the sausage casing and add the sausage meat to the skillet. Using a wooden spoon, break the sausage into little "crumbles." Cook until sausage bits are browned and crunchy. Remove the crumbles from the pan and drain them on paper towels. Discard the garlic cloves.
3. Sprinkle the crumbles onto a parchment-lined cookie sheet. Bake them 15 minutes until the crumbles are dry and firm to the touch.
4. Pack the crumbles in a resealable plastic bag lined with a paper towel. Store them in the refrigerator for up to one week.

Yields 1 cup

2 teaspoons virgin olive oil
3 cloves garlic, whole
¼ pound sweet Italian turkey sausage

Peanut Butter Nibbles

The house brand of shredded wheat is less expensive and usually contains less sugar than the major cereal brands.

Yields 1 cup

¾ cup plain shredded wheat cereal
½ cup natural unsalted peanut butter

1. Place the shredded wheat in a plastic bag and use a rolling pin to crush it into crumbs.
2. Put the peanut butter into a bowl and add the crumbs a few at a time. Mash them into a paste, adding crumbs until mixture is soft but not sticky.
3. Roll the peanut butter crumbs into small balls, about the size of a gumball.
4. Store them in a resealable plastic bag in the refrigerator for up to one week.

Storing Natural Peanut Butter

If you are purchasing natural peanut butter for the first time, you need to mix it prior to eating. This natural "separation" of oil and peanut occurs because there are no added stabilizers. Simply use a butter knife to stir the contents completely. The peanut butter can be stored either at room temperature or in the refrigerator. You won't have to remix it if you keep it chilled.

Kansas City BBQ Beef Tips

Kansas City takes its barbequing so seriously that there is a Kansas City Barbeque Society, which sponsors more than fifty barbecue contests a year.

1. Preheat the oven to 325°F.
2. In a small skillet, heat the olive oil and sauté the garlic over low heat. Add the beef cubes to the skillet and cook till brown and crunchy.
3. Discard the garlic cloves and pat the beef cubes dry with a paper towel. Toss the cubes with the barbecue sauce.
4. Sprinkle the cubes onto a parchment-lined cookie sheet. Bake for 15 minutes until the cubes are dry and firm to the touch.
5. Store in a resealable plastic bag in the refrigerator for up to one week.

Yields 1 cup

1 tablespoon virgin olive cil
3 cloves garlic, whole
¼ pound beef stew meat, chopped into small cubes
2 tablespoons Gates and Sons Bar-B-Q sauce, or any prepared barbecue sauce

Oven-Dried Chicken Shreds

Chicken is one of the most commonly used meats in the world, and no dog would ever turn up his nose if you said, "It tastes just like chicken."

Yields 1 cup

1 boneless chicken breast
2 teaspoons virgin olive oil

Home Dehydration Units

If you want to produce the true leathery texture associated with commercially produced dehydrated chicken or salmon, you can buy a small dehydration machine for under $50. Food dehydrators can dry everything—flowers, fruits, vegetables, and meats. The process can take up to eight hours and reduces the contents by more than half.

1. Preheat the oven to 350°F.
2. Roughly slice the chicken breast into cutlets about ¼-inch thick. Rub the chicken pieces thoroughly with the olive oil.
3. Heat a grill pan and cook the chicken cutlets until they are browned and cooked through, about 5 minutes each side.
4. Using your hands, tear the chicken pieces into shreds. Spread the shredded chicken on a parchment-lined cookie sheet. Bake for 20 minutes until the shreds are dry and firm to the touch.
5. Store them in a resealable plastic bag in the refrigerator for up to one week.

Oven-Baked Egg Strips

*You can substitute any cheese in this recipe, but a hard cheese will work best.
You can even add leftover bits of meat or chicken if you desire.*

1. Preheat the oven to 350°F.
2. Use a fork to scramble the eggs in a glass measuring cup. Add the grated cheese and uncooked rolled oats. Stir until combined.
3. Heat a small skillet at medium-high heat and pour in the egg mixture. Cook the egg mixture without stirring until the eggs are dry and cooked through.
4. Remove the baked-egg pancake from the pan and allow it to cool slightly. Using scissors, cut the egg into thin strips. Spread the egg strips on a parchment-lined cookie sheet. Bake for 20 minutes until strips are dry and firm to the touch.
5. Store them in a resealable plastic bag in the refrigerator for up to one week.

Yields 1 cup

2 organic eggs
1 tablespoon Romano cheese, grated
1 tablespoon old-fashioned rolled oats

Garlic Croutons

Any bread that is thinly sliced for tea sandwiches or is called "cocktail" bread can be used in this recipe. If you can't find it in the bread section of your grocery, look at the deli counter.

Yields 1 cup

¼ cup virgin olive oil
2 cloves garlic, finely minced
3 slices Pepperidge Farm's
    Wheat Bread, thinly sliced
2 tablespoons Romano
    cheese, grated

Heels of Bread

If you don't want to purchase special bread to make these croutons, simply save the heels of the bread you regularly use. It won't matter even if they are stale. If you use Italian bread, the croutons can be a tasty treat for your next salad.

1. Preheat the oven to 350°F.
2. Mix the olive oil and minced garlic in a glass measuring cup. Using a pastry brush or silicone basting brush, brush both sides of the bread with the oil-garlic mixture.
3. Using a serrated knife, cut the bread into strips about ⅜-inch wide. Cut the strips into cubes. Place the bread cubes on a parchment-lined cookie sheet.
4. Bake for 15 minutes till brown and crunchy. Turn off the oven. Sprinkle the cubes with the cheese and toss gently. Return the bread cubes to the oven for another 10 minutes.
5. Store them in a resealable plastic bag at room temperature for one week.

Pasta Crunchies

Pasta contains a high amount of gluten. If your dog has a sensitive digestive system, give him a few pieces to see how he tolerates it.

1. Preheat the oven to 350°F.
2. Boil the pasta in water, but remove the penne one minute before the recommended cooking time.
3. Drain it thoroughly. Place the pasta in a bowl and toss it with the olive oil. Using scissors, cut the penne into bite-size bits. Add the grated Romano cheese and toss until coated.
4. Spread the pasta pieces on a parchment-lined cookie sheet. Bake for 20 minutes until they are dry and firm to the touch.
5. Allow the pieces to cool completely before storing them in a resealable plastic bag. Keep crunchies at room temperature for up to one week.

Yields 1 cup

¾ cup Barilla or De Cecco penne pasta
1 tablespoon virgin olive oil
2 tablespoons Romano cheese, grated

Gluten

Pasta retains its shape and texture even after it is cooked. This is primarily due to its high gluten content. Gluten constitutes about 80 percent of the proteins found in wheat, allowing for the elasticity in dough. Some dogs cannot tolerate gluten. The most common side effects are diarrhea and an upset stomach.

Liverwurst Tidbits

*If you are having trouble administering medicine to your dog,
try concealing it in a piece of liverwurst. Soft and malleable,
the liverwurst will easily hide the tablet.*

Yields 1 cup

¾ cup plain shredded wheat
   cereal
3 ounces Boar's Head
   Liverwurst, room
   temperature
2 ounces cream cheese, room
   temperature

1. Place the shredded wheat in a plastic bag and use a rolling pin to crush it into crumbs.
2. Place the liverwurst and cream cheese on a plate and mash them with a fork until smooth and combined.
3. Pour the shredded wheat crumbs into a bowl. Add the liverwurst–cream cheese mixture to the crumbs. Mix until combined but still soft.
4. Roll the liverwurst mixture into small balls, about the size of a gumball.
5. Store them in a resealable plastic bag in the refrigerator up to one week.

Dried Cinnamon Apples

Orange juice adds a nice sweetness and flavor to the apples, and the acidity will keep the apples from oxidizing and turning brown.

1. Preheat the oven to 350°F.
2. Peel, core, and thinly slice the apples. Toss the slices with the orange juice.
3. Spread the apple slices in a single layer on a parchment-lined cookie sheet. Sprinkle the slices with cinnamon.
4. Bake for 20 minutes until the apples are dry and leathery. Turn the oven off and leave the apples in for another 10 minutes.
5. Allow them to cool completely before placing them in a resealable plastic bag. Store the sliced apples in the refrigerator for up to one week.

Yields 1 cup

1 Granny Smith or Empire apple
½ tablespoon orange juice
2 teaspoons cinnamon

Apples

When selecting apples, choose fruit whose skin is shiny and not dull. Store fruit in the refrigerator to keep it firm and crisp. Washington State produces more than half the apples eaten by Americans.

Chapter 8

Eggs

Eggdrop Oatmeal Soup

If your dog's food bowl is ceramic or metal, place it in the freezer while preparing the soup. The soup will cool on contact, so your dog won't have to wait for her food to cool.

Yields 2 servings, serving size ½ cup

⅓ cup, plus 1 tablespoon organic chicken broth
1 organic egg, beaten
1 tablespoon old-fashioned rolled oats, uncooked
1 tablespoon natural Cheddar cheese, grated

1. In a small saucepan, heat ⅓ cup chicken broth to a low boil.
2. Meanwhile, use a fork to beat the egg in a glass measuring cup with the rolled oats and grated cheese.
3. Pour the egg mixture all at once into the boiling chicken broth, swirling the egg with a fork as it hits the broth. Stir until the egg is cooked and "stringy" looking.
4. Pour the soup into your dog's bowl. To help cool the soup, add the remaining tablespoon of chicken broth to the bowl.

Green Eggs and Ham

If Dr. Seuss had offered his dog a taste of this dish, Sam I Am
would never have had a chance to taste it!

1. Use a fork to the beat the egg in a glass measuring cup. Add the food coloring, chopped broccoli, and Canadian bacon.
2. Heat the canola oil in a small skillet over medium heat.
3. Pour the egg mixture into the skillet all at once. Continue scrambling the egg with a fork as it cooks. Cook until the egg is firm.
4. Add the cooked egg mixture to your dog's bowl. Pour in the chicken broth to help cool the mixture.

Yields 2 servings,
serving size ½ cup

1 organic egg, beaten
2 drops green food coloring
    (optional)
1 tablespoon frozen broccoli,
    chopped and thawed
1 tablespoon Canadian
    bacon, cooked and finely
    chopped, preferably
    Applegate Farms
2 teaspoons canola oil
2 tablespoons organic
    chicken broth, cold

Dr. Seuss

Consisting of only fifty different words, the classic Green Eggs and Ham was first published in 1960 and is the fourth-bestselling children's hardcover book of all time. The book has been translated into numerous languages, including Latin!

Corn and Cheddar Egg Bake

Some dogs are allergic to corn, but those that aren't absolutely love it.

Yields 2 servings,
serving size ½ cup

1 organic egg, beaten
2 tablespoons frozen corn
   niblets, thawed and
   squeezed dry
1 tablespoon natural
   Cheddar cheese, grated
2 tablespoons organic
   chicken broth, cold

1. Use a fork to beat the egg in a glass measuring cup with the corn niblets and grated cheese. Pour the mixture into a buttered ramekin, and cover it loosely with a piece of waxed paper.
2. Cook it in the microwave for 1 minute at medium heat. Check the doneness of the egg and turn the ramekin, cook another 30–45 seconds at medium heat.
3. Add the cooked egg mixture to your dog's bowl. Break the egg apart with a fork and add the chicken broth to help cool the mixture.

Steak and Eggs

*For added flavor use the Kansas City BBQ Beef Tips
on page 91 in place of the steak.*

1. Use a fork to beat the egg in a glass measuring cup. Add the steak and continue beating.
2. Heat the canola oil in a small skillet over medium heat.
3. Pour the egg mixture into the skillet all at once. Continue scrambling the egg with a fork as it cooks. Cook until the egg is firm.
4. Add the cooked egg mixture to your dog's bowl. Pour in the cold broth to help cool the mixture.

Yields 2 servings,
serving size ½ cup

*1 organic egg, beaten
1 tablespoon cooked steak,
  finely chopped
2 teaspoons canola oil
2 tablespoons organic
  chicken broth, cold*

Cast-Iron Skillet
Favored by Southern cooks, cast-iron skillets are workhorses that need to be treated with TLC. Cast-iron skillets need to be properly seasoned prior to initial use, and maintenance includes washing with soapy water while still warm, drying thoroughly, and lightly coating cooking surfaces with cooking oil after each use.

Egg and Sausage Mélange

You can double or triple this recipe and share it with your dog. Just remember to add salt only to your portion and eliminate the chicken broth!

Yields 2 servings,
serving size ½ cup

1 organic egg, beaten
1 tablespoon Romano cheese,
    grated
2 teaspoons virgin olive oil
1 clove garlic, sliced
2 tablespoons cooked Italian
    turkey sausage, casings
    removed
2 tablespoons organic
    chicken broth, cold

1. Use a fork to beat the egg in a glass measuring cup with the grated cheese. Set aside.
2. Heat the olive oil in a small skillet over medium heat and add the sliced garlic. When the garlic is lightly colored, add the cooked sausage meat, breaking it apart with a fork.
3. Pour the egg mixture into the skillet all at once and continue scrambling the egg with a fork as it cooks. Cook until the egg is firm.
4. Add the cooked egg mixture to your dog's bowl. Pour in the cold broth to help cool the mixture.

Flash-Fried Rice and Eggs

Chop or shred your leftover meats and store them in resealable bags in the freezer. If the leftovers have spices or sauces you don't want your dog to eat, simply rinse them with water before storing them.

1. In a small saucepan, heat ⅓ cup chicken broth to a low boil.
2. Meanwhile, use a fork to beat the egg in a glass measuring cup. Pour the egg mixture all at once into the boiling chicken broth, swirling the egg with a fork as it hits the broth. Stir until the egg is cooked and "stringy" looking. Remove the pan from the heat and set it aside.
3. Heat the olive oil in a small skillet over high heat. Add the garlic, rice, and meat all at once, stirring with a wooden spoon. Be careful as the ingredients sizzle and spit.
4. Cook a minute or two, until the rice is crunchy and nicely browned. Remove the skillet from the heat.
5. Add the rice mixture to the egg soup and stir to combine them. Serve alone or over kibble,adding the remaining chicken broth to help cool the mixture.

Yields 2 servings,
serving size ½ cup

⅓ cup plus 2 tablespoons
    organic chicken broth
1 organic egg, beaten
2 teaspoons virgin olive oil
1 clove garlic, minced
2 tablespoons cooked rice
1 tablespoon chopped
    cooked chicken or beef

Flash-Fry

Flash-frying is a new style of cooking where super-high heat is used to stir-fry foods in a flash. Referred to as "explode frying," flash-frying is meant to highlight the natural taste of the food. This method of cooking is especially effective with leafy vegetables.

Eggs Florentine

Traditional Eggs Florentine would involve cracking an egg over a bed of creamed spinach, topping it with cream, and baking it in the oven. This version is faster, easier, and eliminates the cream.

Yields 2 servings,
serving size ½ cup

1 organic egg, beaten
2 tablespoons frozen
    chopped spinach, thawed
    and squeezed dry
1 tablespoon Romano cheese,
    grated
2 tablespoons organic
    chicken broth, cold

1. Use a fork to beat the egg in a glass measuring cup with the chopped spinach and grated cheese. Pour the mixture into a buttered ramekin and cover it loosely with a piece of waxed paper.
2. Cook it in the microwave for 1 minute at medium heat. Check the doneness of the egg and turn the ramekin, and cook another 30–45 seconds at medium heat.
3. Add the cooked egg mixture to your dog's bowl. Break the egg apart with a fork and add the chicken broth to help cool the mixture.

Baked Rice and Eggs

*For variation, you can use brown rice, wild rice, basmati rice,
or even sushi rice for this easy and tasty dish.*

1. Use a fork to beat the egg in a glass measuring cup with the cooked rice, peas, and grated cheese. Pour the mixture into a buttered ramekin, and cover it loosely with a piece of waxed paper.
2. Cook it in the microwave for 1 minute at medium heat. Check the doneness of the egg, and turn the ramekin, cook it another 30–45 seconds at medium heat.
3. Add the cooked egg mixture to your dog's bowl. Break the egg apart with a fork, and add the chicken broth to help cool the mixture.

Yields 2 servings,
serving size ½ cup

1 organic egg, beaten
2 tablespoons cooked rice
1 tablespoon frozen peas,
    rinsed under hot water
1 tablespoon natural
    Cheddar cheese, grated
2 tablespoons organic
    chicken broth, cold

Brown Rice

Sometimes referred to as "hulled rice," brown rice has a mild nutty flavor and is chewier than white rice. Brown rice retains more vitamins and dietary minerals because only the husk is removed. To produce white rice, however, both the husk and the bran layer underneath are removed. Brown rice offers the added benefit of helping to lower LDL cholesterol.

Scalloped Eggs and Bacon

If you do not eat pork, turkey bacon is a great substitute. With less fat and more meat per slice, it is a healthy choice to make for everyone in your family.

**Yields 2 servings,
serving size ½ cup**

*1 hard-boiled organic egg
1 tablespoon, preferably
   Applegate Farms Sunday
   bacon, cooked and
   crumbled
1 tablespoon frozen peas,
   rinsed under hot water
1 tablespoon natural
   Cheddar cheese, grated
2 tablespoons organic
   chicken broth, cold*

1. Use a fork to mash the egg as if preparing egg salad. Toss with the bacon, peas, and grated cheese.
2. Place the mixture into a buttered ramekin, and cover it loosely with a piece of waxed paper. Cook it in the microwave for 30 seconds at medium heat or until the cheese is melted.
3. Add the cooked egg mixture to your dog's bowl. Break the egg apart with a fork, and add the chicken broth to help cool the mixture.

Ruby Hard-Boiled Eggs

Hard-boiled eggs combined with pickled beets and onion are a classic New York City delicatessen offering. Here, only the ingredients dogs love are used for this take on a NYC classic.

1. Use a fork to mash the egg as if preparing egg salad. Toss the egg with the beets and peas. Don't worry about the eggs turning pink—that's supposed to happen.
2. Add the cooked egg mixture to your dog's bowl and stir in the chicken broth if desired. Serve it alone or over kibble.

Yields 2 servings, serving size ½ cup

1 hard-boiled organic egg
2 tablespoons cooked beets, finely chopped
1 tablespoon frozen peas, rinsed under hot water
2 tablespoons organic chicken broth (optional)

Classic Hard-Boiled Eggs

The boiled egg is easy to prepare and requires only a few simple steps. Place the eggs in a saucepan and cover them with cold tap water. Bring them to a rolling boil over high heat. Once the water reaches a rolling boil, reduce the heat and cook for 10 minutes. Remove the eggs from the heat and place them in ice water for a few minutes. Store hard-boiled eggs in the refrigerator until you're ready to eat them.

Microwaved Eggs with Dried Anchovies

Microwaving eggs is an easy and fast cooking method when you're pressed for time. Remember to turn your dish halfway through the cooking process, and always have potholders at the ready.

Yields 2 servings, serving size ½ cup

1 organic egg, beaten
2 tablespoons wild rice
2 tablespoons cooked beef, finely chopped
1 tablespoon dried anchovies, finely ground
¼ cup plus 2 tablespoons organic chicken broth

1. Using a fork, beat the egg until it is light and fluffy. Combine it with the rice, chopped beef, and dried anchovies. Set the mixture aside.
2. Pour ¼ cup chicken broth into a microwavable bowl and microwave the broth on high for 3 minutes. Be careful when removing the bowl from the microwave; it will be hot. Pour in the egg mixture and whisk it with a fork. Return it to the microwave for another minute. The egg will be puffy and will float in the bowl. Remove it from the microwave and continually stir the egg with a fork to break it apart.
3. Add the cooked egg mixture to your dog's bowl. Add the remaining cold chicken broth to help cool the mixture.

Chapter 9

Chicken and Turkey

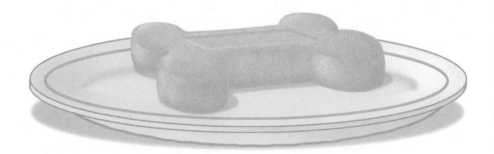

Arroz con Pollo

Saffron, one of the most expensive spices, gives this traditional Latin favorite
its yellow golden color. Turmeric, a spice from the ginger family,
is an economical substitution.

Yields 32 servings,
serving size 2 tablespoons

1 2½- to 3-pound broiler
    chicken
2 tablespoons virgin olive oil
1 cup long-grain rice, cooked
1 bay leaf
2 cloves garlic
1 16-ounce carton organic
    chicken broth
1 7½-ounce can diced
    tomatoes
½ cup frozen peas
Pinch saffron threads
    (optional)

1. Rinse the chicken thoroughly and pat dry with paper towels. Cut it up into large pieces.
2. Heat the olive oil in a heavy skillet and brown the chicken pieces on all sides. Turn the pieces when they no longer stick to the pan. Remove the chicken.
3. Add the rice, bay leaf, and garlic to the skillet and sauté until rice is golden and translucent. Add the chicken broth and the can of tomatoes (do not drain it first); bring the mixture to a boil. Arrange the chicken on top of the rice mixture. Cover and simmer 30–35 minutes until the chicken is tender.
4. Stir in the peas and saffron (if desired). Remove the skillet from the heat. When the chicken is cool enough to handle, remove and discard the skin and bones. Tear the meat into bite-size pieces and add it back to the stew mixture. Serve over kibble.

Chicken and Roasted Vegetables

Don't scrub away the brown bits left over when you cook or brown meats. If you add water to a hot skillet or roasting pan, you have the fastest and easiest kibble "gravy" possible.

1. Preheat the oven to 350°F. Rinse the chicken, pat it dry with paper towels, and place it in a baking dish.
2. Add the remaining ingredients and gently stir to coat chicken and vegetables. Cover the dish tightly with foil. Pierce the foil with a knife to allow the steam to escape.
3. Place it in the oven and bake for 40 minutes. Remove the foil, stir the mixture gently, and return the dish to the oven for another 15 minutes or until the vegetables and chicken are browned and nicely crusted.
4. When the chicken is cool enough to handle, tear it into bite-size pieces and add it back to the vegetable mixture. Serve it over kibble with a little extra chicken broth.

Yields 16 servings, serving size 2 tablespoons

3 chicken thighs, skin removed
2 tablespoons virgin olive oil
2 cloves garlic, sliced into chunks
¼ cup frozen peas, rinsed under hot water
2 red potatoes, scrubbed and cut in chunks
1 carrot, peeled and cut into discs
2 tablespoons organic chicken broth

Free-Range Chickens

Many small poultry farmers are raising free-range chickens. These birds are free of anti-biotics, eat vegetarian feed, roam freely in a farm environment, and are supported by ranchers who use sustainable farming methods. The chickens make for more flavorful and healthier eating.

Chicken Cacciatore

A traditional Italian chicken dish, cacciatore is referred to as "hunter style."
Cacciatore is an Italian word meaning "hunter."

Yields 16 servings,
serving size 2 tablespoons

3 chicken thighs, skin
   removed
2 tablespoons unbleached
   flour
1 tablespoon virgin olive oil
2 cloves garlic, sliced into
   chunks
1 carrot, peeled and finely
   chopped
¼ cup crushed tomatoes
2 tablespoons organic
   chicken broth

1. Rinse the chicken and pat it dry with paper towels. Spread the flour on a piece of waxed paper, and coat the thighs thoroughly.
2. Heat the olive oil in a heavy skillet over medium-high heat. Add the chicken pieces and cook until they are browned and a nice crust has formed. Turn the chicken when it no longer sticks to the pan. Remove the chicken to a plate.
3. Use a wooden spoon to scrape the brown bits off the bottom of the pan, and add the garlic and carrots. Cook until the vegetables are soft and caramelized. Add the crushed tomatoes and chicken broth. Return the chicken pieces and any juices to the skillet. Lower the heat, cover, and cook at a gentle simmer for 20 minutes, stirring occasionally to make sure the chicken doesn't stick and the tomatoes don't burn.
4. If the sauce is too thin, remove the cover and cook for a few minutes to thicken. When chicken is cool enough to handle, tear it into bite-size pieces and add them back to the tomato mixture. Serve over kibble with a little extra chicken broth.

Chicken Stew

To remove the chicken's slimy layer, place the whole chicken in a stockpot, cover it with water, and add 2 tablespoons of kosher salt. Allow the chicken to soak for up to 20 minutes and then rinse it thoroughly.

1. Rinse the chicken thoroughly, place it in a heavy stockpot and add the carton of chicken broth and the bay leaf. If the chicken is not fully submerged, add water. Cover the pot, bring the water to a boil, and reduce the heat to a simmer.
2. While the chicken is simmering, heat the olive oil in a heavy skillet over medium-high heat. Add the garlic and carrots. Cook for 3 minutes, stirring with a wooden spoon. Add the remaining 2 tablespoons chicken broth and the peas. Whisk in the flour as the broth thickens.
3. Add a ladle of the liquid from the stockpot to the skillet and whisk until thoroughly combined.
4. Add the vegetable mixture to the stockpot. Cover and continue cooking at a low simmer for 2 hours or until the chicken is tender. Allow to cool.
5. When the chicken is cool enough to handle, remove and discard the skin and bones. Tear the meat into bite-size pieces and add it back to the stew mixture. Serve over kibble.

Yields 24 servings, serving size 2 tablespoons

1 3-pound organic chicken
1 16-ounce carton plus 2 tablespoons organic chicken broth
1 bay leaf
1 tablespoon virgin olive oil
2 cloves garlic, sliced
2 carrots, peeled and chopped
¼ cup frozen peas
1 tablespoon flour

Why No Onions?

Onions can be toxic to dogs. They cause Heinz body anemia. Heinz bodies are small bubble-like projections that protrude from red blood cells, creating a weak spot in the cells that makes them susceptible to rupture. If numerous blood cells rupture, anemia can result and can be life threatening in severe cases.

Chicken Stroganoff

Traditionally, sour cream is added to this rich and tasty dish. Adding plain yogurt instead retains the creaminess but eliminates the richness of sour cream.

Yields 24 servings, serving size 2 tablespoons

1 organic chicken breast, cut up
1 tablespoon unbleached flour
1 tablespoon virgin olive oil
2 cloves garlic, sliced
½ cup frozen chopped broccoli, thawed
¼ cup plus 2 tablespoons organic chicken broth
½ cup nonfat plain yogurt

1. Rinse the chicken and pat it dry with paper towels. Spread the flour on a piece of waxed paper and coat the chicken pieces thoroughly.
2. Heat the olive oil in a heavy skillet over medium-high heat. Add the chicken pieces and cook until they are browned and a nice crust has formed. Turn the chicken when it no longer sticks to the pan. Remove the chicken to a plate.
3. Use a wooden spoon to scrape up the brown bits and add the garlic and broccoli. Sauté for 2 minutes, stirring with a wooden spoon. Add the chicken broth and stir as the broth thickens. Return the chicken pieces and any juices to the skillet. Add the nonfat yogurt.
4. Lower the heat, cover, and cook at a gentle simmer for 20 minutes, stirring occasionally.
5. Remove from the heat. When the chicken is cool enough to handle, tear it into bite-size pieces and add it back to the yogurt mixture. Serve over kibble with 2 tablespoons chicken broth.

Wild Rice and Grilled Chicken

Cook the rice in chicken broth rather than water for added flavor.
Salt is unnecessary when preparing rice for your dog.

1. Heat a grill pan over medium heat. Toss the sliced chicken breast in the olive oil and place them on the hot grill pan. Do not turn the pieces until the chicken has grill marks and no longer sticks to the pan. If the chicken sticks, allow it to cook a minute longer.

2. When the chicken is cool enough to handle, shred it into bite-size pieces and toss it with the cooked wild rice. Add the chicken broth and serve over kibble.

Yields 8 servings, serving size ¼ cup

1 chicken breast, cut into thick slices
2 teaspoons virgin olive oil
1 cup wild rice, cooked
2 tablespoons organic chicken broth

Grilled Chicken with Pesto

Grill some extra chicken for your family, and as soon as you remove it from the grill pan, spread a spoonful of prepared pesto on each piece. Serve it on a bed of mixed greens with sliced tomatoes and fresh mozzarella. Add a generous drizzle of virgin olive oil and a few twists from a pepper mill and you have a quick, easy, and tasty supper.

Skewered Turkey and Sweet Potato

Traditionally served as part of a full English breakfast, orange marmalade has a sweet and bitter tang that is thought to calm an upset stomach.

Yields 24 servings,
serving size 2 tablespoons

1 turkey breast
1 sweet potato, boiled and
    cooled
1 tablespoon canola oil
½ apple, peeled and cut into
    chunks
1 tablespoon orange juice
1 tablespoon prepared
    barbecue sauce
1 tablespoon orange
    marmalade
2 tablespoons organic
    chicken broth

1. Rinse the turkey breast and pat it dry with paper towels. Cut it into large cubes and place them in a shallow bowl. Peel the cooked sweet potato and cut it into 1-inch chunks. Add them to the turkey and toss with canola oil. Add the apple chunks and orange juice. Let rest for 20 minutes.

2. Preheat the broiler and move the oven rack to the uppermost rung. Thread the turkey, sweet potato, and apple on skewers. Spray a foil-lined pan with cooking spray. Place the skewers on the pan and broil 4 minutes each side.

3. Mix the barbecue sauce and marmalade in a measuring cup. Brush the skewers with the orange barbecue sauce and return them to the oven. Grill 3–5 minutes longer on each side.

4. When the skewers are cool enough to handle, remove the turkey, potatoes, and apples. Shred the turkey into bite-size pieces, and use a fork to break up the potatoes and apples. Serve over kibble with 2 tablespoons chicken broth.

Easy Turkey Burgers

These miniburgers make great snacks at a dog's birthday party. Serve them on dinner rolls, which are just the right size for the tiny patties.

1. Use your hands to mix the turkey meat with the beaten egg and minced garlic. Add the rolled oats and grated cheese. Wet your hands and form them into small silver dollar–size patties.
2. Heat a grill pan over medium heat. Lightly spray it with nonstick spray. Grill the burgers 5 minutes on each side. When they are cool enough to handle, break them apart with a fork. Add the chicken broth and serve over kibble.

Yields 16 servings, serving size 2 tablespoons

8 ounces ground turkey meat
1 organic egg, beaten
1 clove garlic, minced
2 tablespoons old-fashioned rolled oats
2 tablespoons Romano cheese, grated
2 tablespoons organic chicken broth, cold

Burger Condiments

If you end up serving the burgers at your dog's birthday, remember to offer toppings cut to the appropriate size. You might consider a dollop of bleu cheese, the Barbeque Sauce on page 194, or a schmear of liver and cream cheese pâté, especially for the birthday boy or girl.

BBQ Chicken

Save some of this easy barbecued chicken for
Barbecued Chicken in a Biscuit, page 36.

Yields 16 servings,
serving size 2 tablespoons

1 chicken breast, cut into
thick slices
2 teaspoons virgin olive oil
2 tablespoons barbecue
sauce
2 tablespoons organic
chicken broth

1. Heat a grill pan over medium heat. Toss the sliced chicken breast in the olive oil and place it on the hot grill pan. Do not turn the pieces until the chicken has grill marks and no longer sticks to the pan. If the chicken sticks, allow it to cook a minute longer.

2. Remove the chicken to a plate and toss it with the barbecue sauce. When the chicken is cool enough to handle, shred it into bite-size pieces. Add the chicken broth and serve it over kibble.

Boiled Chicken Gizzards

When you buy a whole roasting chicken, the neck, gizzard, and sometimes the giblets come tucked inside, wrapped in parchment-type paper. Rather than throwing them out, boil them to make a delectable dinner for your dog.

1. Remove the parchment wrappers and rinse the neck, gizzards, and giblets under cool water. Place them in a heavy pot and cover them with cold water. Add the bay leaves and garlic cloves and bring to a boil. Once the water reaches a boil, lower the heat to simmer, cover, and cook for 40 minutes.

2. Remove the chicken parts from the water and allow them to cool. Pick the meat off the neck bones, roughly chop the gizzard and giblets, and store them in a plastic container with some of the cooking water. Serve over kibble.

Yields 16 servings, serving size 2 tablespoons

1 chicken's neck, giblets, and gizzard
2 bay leaves
2 cloves garlic

Gizzards

Found in other animals besides birds, a gizzard is a specialized stomach with a thick, muscular wall used for grinding food. Popular throughout Asia, grilled chicken gizzards are sold as street food in South Korea, China, Taiwan, Japan, and the Philippines. Stewed gizzards are eaten as a snack in Portugal, while pickled turkey gizzards are a traditional food in some parts of the American Midwest. In the South, the gizzard is served fried and sometimes eaten with hot or honey mustard sauce.

Chicken Biscuit Casserole

From the French for "stew pan," casseroles sometimes receive negative culinary press. Many nationalities have their own version of these one-dish comfort meals. Just avoid using canned soups and "flavor packets," as many of them are loaded with excess amounts of salt and MSG.

Yields 32 servings,
serving size 2 tablespoons

1 cup cooked chicken breast,
   shredded
½ cup Savory Chicken and
   Vegetable Biscuits, page
   55, crumbled
½ cup long-grain rice, cooked
¼ cup corn niblets
¼ cup natural Colby cheese,
   grated
1 7½-ounce can diced
   tomatoes
2 tablespoons organic
   chicken broth

1. Preheat the oven to 350°F.
2. Combine all the ingredients, except the chicken broth in a bowl; then transfer the contents to a shallow casserole dish. Sprinkle with a little extra cheese and cover with foil. Bake for 15 minutes until it becomes hot and bubbly. Remove the foil and bake for a few minutes longer or till a nice crust forms.
3. Allow to cool slightly. Serve with chicken broth over kibble.

Chicken Gumbo

You can always start with broth made from your Thanksgiving turkey carcass; freeze it in ice-cube trays and you have the right portion.

1. Rinse the chicken thoroughly, place it in a heavy stockpot and add the carton of chicken broth and the bay leaf. Add water if necessary, so the chicken is completely submerged in liquid. Cover, bring to a boil, and reduce heat to a simmer.
2. While the chicken is simmering, cook the sausage in a heavy skillet over medium-high heat. Add the olive oil, garlic, and corn. Cook for 2 minutes, stirring with a wooden spoon. Whisk in the flour and continue stirring as the mixture thickens. Add the 2 tablespoons of chicken broth and the tomatoes.
3. Add the tomato, vegetable, and sausage mixture to the stockpot. Continue cooking, covered, at a low simmer for 2 hours or until the chicken is tender. Allow it to cool.
4. When the chicken is cool enough to handle, remove and discard the skin and bones. Tear the meat into bite-size pieces and add it back to the stew mixture. Stir in the cooked rice and serve it over kibble.

Yields 24 servings, serving size 2 tablespoons

1 3-pound organic chicken
1 16-ounce carton plus 2 tablespoons organic chicken broth
1 bay leaf
1 link Applegate Farms natural smoked sausage, casing removed and crumbled
2 teaspoons virgin olive oil
2 cloves garlic
½ cup corn niblets
1 tablespoon flour
½ cup crushed tomatoes
1 cup cooked brown rice

Okra

Used as a key thickening ingredient in gumbo, okra is a green pod-shaped vegetable filled with many seeds; it is grown in tropical and temperate climates. *Okra* is also the West African word for gumbo. Okra can be used as a thickener or eaten steamed, stir-fried, deep fried, or even pickled.

Easy Chicken Parmigiana Tenders

If you have leftover egg after you've prepared the chicken, you can use it to make egg fritters. Add more biscuit crumbs and grated cheese to the egg until it is thick as custard. Stir the mixture with a fork. Spoon it into hot oil. Cook the egg fritters until they're firm and nicely browned.

Yields 16 servings

½ cup Roasted Tomato and Mozzarella Biscotti, page 77, crushed
¼ cup Pecorino Romano cheese, grated
2 chicken breasts, cut into thick slices
1 organic egg, beaten
2 tablespoons virgin olive oil
2 teaspoons organic chicken broth

1. Mix the crushed biscotti and grated Romano cheese on a piece of waxed paper. Dip the chicken slices in the beaten egg and then in the biscotti and cheese crumbs.

2. Heat the olive oil in a heavy saucepan over medium heat. Add the chicken pieces to the hot oil in a single layer and sauté till deep brown. Turn the pieces when the chicken no longer sticks to the pan. If the chicken sticks, allow it to cook a minute longer.

3. Remove the chicken to a paper towel–lined plate and allow it to cool. Chop the chicken tenders into bite-size pieces. Add the chicken broth and serve over kibble.

Chapter 10
Meats

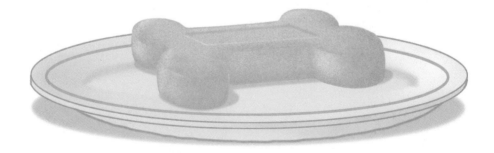

BBQ Beef Stew

Be the first on your block to offer your dog a beef stew smoothie. Process the cooked stew in a blender or a food processor, adding additional water or organic beef broth until you get the perfect consistency.

Yields 16 servings,
serving size 2 tablespoons

1 tablespoon virgin olive oil
2 cloves garlic, chopped
6 ounces beef stew meat
2 tablespoons unbleached
*   flour*
2 tablespoons tomato paste
1 teaspoon ground ginger
2 cups organic beef broth
½ cup sweet potato, cooked
*   and mashed*

1. In a heavy skillet, heat the olive oil and sauté the garlic until light brown. Cut the stew meat into bite-size bits. Spread the flour on a piece of waxed paper and thoroughly coat each cube of meat with flour. Raise the heat to medium-high and sauté the beef cubes until they have a nice brown crust on all sides, about 5 minutes.

2. Add the tomato paste and ginger and cook for another minute. Add the beef broth, stirring to combine, and bring to a boil. Lower the heat, cover, and simmer for 40 minutes, stirring occasionally.

3. Transfer 1 cup of the stew to a food processor and add the cooked sweet potato. Process until smooth and creamy, adding a bit more beef broth if the mixture is too thick. Return the puréed beef stew to the pot and stir until combined. Serve over kibble, thinning with more beef broth if desired.

Braised Pork with Sweet Potato, Apples, and Ginger

This recipe combines three types of ginger: ground, fresh, and crystallized. Ginger adds a savory flavor, aids in digestion, and helps settle upset stomachs.

1. In a heavy skillet, heat the olive oil and sauté the garlic until light brown. Cut the pork cubes into bite-size bits. Spread the flour on a piece of waxed paper and thoroughly coat each cube of meat with flour. Raise the heat to medium-high and sauté the pork cubes till they have a nice brown crust on all sides, about 5 minutes.

2. Add the apples and three types of ginger. Cook until caramelized, about 5 minutes. Add the chicken broth, stirring to combine, and bring to a boil. Lower the heat, cover, and simmer for 40 minutes, stirring occasionally.

3. Gently stir in the cooked sweet potato. Continue stirring as sauce thickens and bubbles. Serve over kibble, thinning with more chicken broth if desired.

Yields 16 servings, serving size 2 tablespoons

1 tablespoon virgin olive oil
2 cloves garlic, chopped
6 ounces pork cubes
2 tablespoons unbleached flour
1 apple, chopped
1 teaspoon ground ginger
1 teaspoon fresh ginger, grated
1 teaspoon crystallized ginger, finely chopped
2 cups organic chicken broth
½ cup sweet potato, cooked and mashed

Ginger

With a pungent taste and a spicy sweet aroma, ginger is a popular flavoring for candy, cookies, cakes, and beverages. Young ginger roots are juicy and fleshy with a mild taste, and mature ginger roots are fibrous and dry.

Sauerbraten

Sauerbraten comes from the German words sauer, *meaning "sour," and* braten, *meaning "roast meat." Traditionally, sauerbraten is marinated in vinegar with cloves and sugar beet syrup and served with a sauce made with gingerbread.*

Yields 16 servings,
serving size 2 tablespoons

1 tablespoon virgin olive oil
2 cloves garlic, chopped
6 ounces beef stew meat
2 tablespoons unbleached
    flour
2 beets, chopped
¼ teaspoon ground ginger
2 cups organic beef broth
½ cup Almond and Ginger
    Biscuits, page 49
½ cup sweet potato, cooked
    and mashed

1. In a heavy skillet, heat the olive oil and sauté the garlic till light brown. Cut the stew meat into bite-size bits. Spread the flour on a piece of waxed paper and thoroughly coat each cube of meat with flour. Raise the heat to medium-high and sauté the beef cubes till they have a nice brown crust on all sides, about 5 minutes.

2. Add the beets and ginger. Cook until caramelized, about 5 minutes. Add the beef broth, stirring to combine, and bring to a boil. Lower the heat, cover, and simmer for 40 minutes, stirring occasionally.

3. Break the Almond and Ginger Biscuits into bite-size pieces and add to the sauerbraten. Continue stirring as sauce thickens and bubbles. Gently stir in the cooked sweet potato. Serve over kibble, thinning with more beef broth if desired.

Beef Pot Roast

Pot roast can be cooked on the stove, in the oven, or in a slow cooker.

1. In a heavy skillet, heat the olive oil and sauté the garlic till light brown. Cut the stew meat into bite-size bits. Spread the flour on a piece of waxed paper and thoroughly coat each cube of meat with flour. Raise the heat to medium-high and sauté the beef cubes until they have a nice brown crust on all sides, about 5 minutes.

2. Add the carrots. Cook until caramelized, about 5 minutes. Add the beef broth, stirring to combine, and bring to a boil. Lower the heat, cover, and simmer for 40 minutes, stirring occasionally.

3. Transfer 1 cup of the stew to a food processor and add the cooked sweet potato and drained chopped spinach. Process till smooth and creamy, adding a bit more beef broth if the mixture is too thick. Return puréed beef stew to the pot and stir until combined. Serve over kibble, thinning with more beef broth if desired.

Yields 16 servings, serving size 2 tablespoons

1 tablespoon virgin olive oil
2 cloves garlic, chopped
6 ounces beef stew meat
2 tablespoons unbleached flour
2 carrots, chopped
2 cups organic beef broth
½ cup sweet potato, cooked and mashed
½ cup frozen chopped spinach, thawed

Pot Roasts

Pot roasts have been around since the 1800s. Roasts are made with meat from the chuck portion of a cow, the shoulder meat. This meat is very tough, and the method of cooking it in a pot with liquids and vegetables makes it tender and gives it flavor.

Beef and Vegetable Stir-Fry

Even if you don't have a wok, you can still whip up this quick and easy recipe using a deep-sided skillet. Allow the skillet to get very hot and keep the food moving throughout the cooking process.

- -

Yields 16 servings,
serving size 2 tablespoons

1 tablespoon virgin olive oil
2 cloves garlic, chopped
6 ounces beef stew meat
2 carrots, finely chopped
*½ cup broccoli, finely
    chopped*
*½ cup cauliflower, finely
    chopped*
½ cup organic beef broth
½ cup brown rice, cooked

1. In a heavy skillet, heat the olive oil and sauté the garlic till light brown. Cut the stew meat into bite-size bits. Raise the heat to medium-high and sauté the beef cubes until they have a nice brown crust on all sides, about 5 minutes.
2. Add the carrots, broccoli, and cauliflower and continue cooking for 2 minutes, constantly stirring with a wooden spoon. Make sure the vegetables remain crisp.
3. Add the beef broth and stir in the cooked rice. Transfer 1 cup of the stew to a food processor and process till smooth. Combine with the rice and remaining stew. Serve over kibble, thinning with more beef broth if desired.

Savory Short Ribs

The longer you cook the ribs, the deeper the flavor, and the easier it will be to remove the meat from the bone.

1. In a heavy skillet, heat the olive oil and sauté the garlic till light brown. Spread the flour on a piece of waxed paper and thoroughly coat each rib with flour. Raise the heat to medium-high and sauté the short ribs until they have a nice brown crust on all sides, about 5 minutes.

2. Add the carrots and apples. Cook until caramelized, about 5 minutes. Add the beef broth, stirring to combine. Bring to a boil. Lower the heat, cover, and simmer for 1 hour, stirring occasionally. Add the molasses and cook for another 15 minutes until thickened and bubbly.

3. Remove the short ribs. When they are cool enough to handle, carefully remove the meat from the bones. Return the meat to the pot and stir till combined. Serve over kibble, thinning with more beef broth if desired.

Yields 16 servings, serving size 2 tablespoons

1 tablespoon virgin olive oil
2 cloves garlic, chopped
2 tablespoons unbleached flour
2 pounds short ribs
2 carrots, chopped
½ cup sliced apple
2 cups organic beef broth
1 tablespoon molasses

Give a Dog a Bone

Dogs love bones, but be careful when giving your dog real bones. Bones that are too small can get lodged in the throat or intestine, causing choking or blockages. Bones that are too brittle can shatter and damage the digestive tract.

Asian-Style Beef Tips

If you want a quick meal for your family, marinate the pepper steak in a mixture of olive oil, salt and pepper, garlic, and lime juice. Fry some green and red pepper strips and onions, and grill the steak strips. Serve wrapped in warm flour tortillas, and you have your own homemade fajitas.

**Yields 16 servings,
serving size 2 tablespoons**

2 cloves garlic, chopped
1 teaspoon ground ginger
½ tablespoon virgin olive oil
½ lime, juiced
½ pound pepper steak
½ cup organic beef broth
½ cup brown rice, cooked

1. Combine the garlic, ginger, olive oil, and lime juice in a small plastic container. Add the pepper steak strips, cover, and marinate in the refrigerator for as little as 20 minutes or as long as overnight.
2. Heat a grill pan until hot but not smoking. Remove the steak strips from the marinade and cook on the grill for about 3 minutes per side. Discard the marinade.
3. Remove the cooked beef strips and chop them into bite-size bits. Combine the cut-up beef with the beef broth and rice. Serve over kibble, thinning with more beef broth if desired.

Meat Loaf

You can double or triple the recipe and freeze the uncooked loaves. Wrap them in plastic wrap, pack them in a labeled and dated resealable plastic bag, and you have meals ready for the month.

1. Heat the oven to 350°F.
2. Soak the kibble in the beef broth in a small bowl until it turns to mush. Add the beaten egg, ground beef, shredded carrots, and cooked rice. Use your hands or a spatula to mix the ingredients thoroughly.
3. Pat the ground beef mixture into a small loaf shape and place in a shallow baking pan. Bake for 35 minutes until nicely browned but still moist.
4. Slice the meat loaf and use a fork to break it apart. Serve it over kibble, thinning with more beef broth if desired.

Yields 16 servings, serving size 2 tablespoons

½ cup kibble
½ cup organic beef broth
1 organic egg, beaten
½ pound lean ground beef
2 carrots, shredded
½ cup brown rice, cooked

Blue-Plate Special

Meat loaf is one of the classic staples of the blue-plate special. Culinary lore records that the term *blue-plate special* was used to refer to items offered at Fred Harvey restaurants in the early 1890s. Fred Harvey's restaurants were built at train stations, and the blue-plate specials were designed to feed hungry travelers who had only a few minutes between trains.

Texas-Style Beef Skillet

If your dog can't tolerate corn, you can substitute cooked rice, couscous, pasta, or even mashed potato. And of course you can substitute chicken, turkey, lamb, or pork for the beef.

Yields 16 servings, serving size 2 tablespoons

½ pound lean ground beef
3 cloves garlic, finely chopped
1 cup corn niblets
½ cup crushed tomatoes

1. In a heavy skillet, sauté the ground beef and garlic until the meat is browned and no longer pink. Drain any fat from the pan.
2. Place the corn and crushed tomatoes in a food processor and pulse two or three times. Add the corn-tomato mixture to the cooked beef, stirring to combine.
3. Serve over kibble, thinning with beef broth if desired.

BBQ Buffalo Burgers

Bison meat is very lean and a good choice for dogs that need to watch their fat intake. Cook at a lower temperature than you would beef, turn the burgers only once, and coat your grill with cooking spray or olive oil. Serve rare or medium rare; otherwise the meat will dry out.

1. Heat the oven to 350°F.
2. Soak the biscuits in the beef broth in a small bowl until they turn to mush. Add the beaten egg, ground bison, bleu cheese, and barbecue sauce. Use your hands or a spatula to mix ingredients thoroughly.
3. Pat the ground bison mixture into small burgers and grill for about 3 minutes per side.
4. Use a fork to break the burgers apart and serve over kibble, thinning with more beef broth if desired.

Yields 16 servings, serving size 2 tablespoons

½ cup Bleu Cheese and
    Tomato Biscuits, page 54
¼ cup organic beef broth
1 organic egg, beaten
½ pound ground bison
1 tablespoon bleu cheese,
    crumbled
2 tablespoons prepared
    barbecue sauce

The Skinny on Bison

Compared to other meats, bison packs more protein and nutrients. It contains about four times less fat than beef or pork and about three times less fat than chicken. Bison are generally not subjected to hormones or antibiotics and are strictly grass fed. Bison is a rich, filling meat that has a slightly sweet taste.

Venison and Apples

Venison comes from either farm-raised or wild deer and is sometimes sold frozen. When purchasing venison meat, select meat that is darker in color and has finely grained flesh and white fat. Venison is highly perishable, so it is best to use it within two days of purchase and freeze any leftovers.

Yields 16 servings,
serving size 2 tablespoons

1 tablespoon virgin olive oil
4 cloves garlic, chopped
2 tablespoons unbleached flour
½ pound venison steak, cut into cubes
2 carrots, chopped
½ cup sliced apple
1 cup organic beef broth

1. In a heavy skillet, heat the olive oil and sauté the garlic till light brown. Spread the flour on a piece of waxed paper and thoroughly coat each venison cube with flour. Raise the heat to medium-high and sauté the venison cubes until they have a nice brown crust on all sides, about 5 minutes.
2. Add the carrots and apples. Cook until caramelized, about 5 minutes. Add the beef broth, stirring to combine, and bring to a boil. Lower the heat, and simmer until thickened and bubbly.
3. Serve over kibble, thinning with more beef broth if desired.

Venison

High in protein and low in saturated fat, venison is also a great source of iron—perfect for dogs that are pregnant or lactating. Venison has less fat and fewer calories than beef and is a good source of vitamin B12, riboflavin, and vitamin B6, all of which help with improving cardiovascular health and energy.

Venison Liver and Bacon

Venison liver should be well cleaned and should not contain any spots or discolorations. Soaking it in milk or water helps remove excess blood. Change the liquid several times and allow the liver to soak for at least 2 hours.

- -

1. Soak liver cubes in milk or water for at least 2 hours, changing the liquid periodically. Drain the cubes and pat them dry with a paper towel. Cut the bacon into 1-inch pieces. Add the bacon and garlic to a hot skillet and sauté till the garlic turns light brown.
2. Spread the flour on a piece of waxed paper and thoroughly coat each venison cube with flour. Raise the heat to medium-high and sauté the venison cubes until they have a nice brown crust on all sides, about 5 minutes.
3. Drain the fat from the pan and mix in the wild rice and beef broth. Serve over kibble, thinning with more beef broth if desired.

Yields 16 servings, serving size 2 tablespoons

½ pound venison liver, cut into cubes
1 cup organic milk
1 slice nitrite-free/nitrate-free bacon, preferably Applegate Farms
4 cloves garlic, chopped
2 tablespoons unbleached flour
1 cup wild rice, cooked
¼ cup organic beef broth

Scissors in the Kitchen

Even if you don't own a pair of kitchen shears, a pair of regular scissors can come in very handy. Use scissors to cut meats, bacon, pasta, pizza, and fresh herbs. If all else fails, they're perfect for opening stubborn bags and packages. Wash them thoroughly after each use, and run them through your dishwasher at least once a week.

Lamb Cubes with Parsley and Mint

Lamb offers an earthy, moist flavor, and it marries well with garlic, mint, and parsley. As lamb is readily available, it is often recommended for dogs whose digestive systems are sensitive to beef and chicken.

- -

Yields 16 servings, serving size 2 tablespoons

1 tablespoon virgin olive oil
4 cloves garlic, chopped
½ pound lamb cubes
2 tablespoons unbleached flour
1 cup organic vegetable broth
¼ cup Italian parsley, chopped
2 tablespoons fresh mint, chopped
½ cup long-grain rice, cooked

1. In a heavy skillet, heat the olive oil and sauté the garlic till light brown. Cut the lamb cubes into bite-size bits. Spread the flour on a piece of waxed paper and thoroughly coat each cube of meat with flour. Raise the heat to medium-high and sauté the lamb cubes until they have a nice brown crust on all sides, about 5 minutes.

2. Add the vegetable broth, stirring to combine, and bring to a boil. Lower the heat, cover, and simmer for 40 minutes, stirring occasionally.

3. Transfer 1 cup of the stew to a food processor and add the parsley and mint. Process until smooth and creamy, adding a bit more vegetable broth if the mixture is too thick. Return puréed lamb mixture to the skillet, add the cooked rice, and stir until combined. Serve over kibble, thinning with more vegetable broth if desired.

Ground Pork and Lamb Patties

Pine nuts, also known as pignoli in Italian, are the edible seeds of pine trees. Pine nuts contain the highest protein level of any nut and are also a good source of fiber. Look for them in Italian markets and in Middle Eastern groceries. Keep them refrigerated. Once opened, pine nuts can turn rancid quickly.

1. Combine the egg, pork, lamb, parsley, mint, pine nuts, and rice in a bowl. Use your hands or a spatula to mix all ingredients thoroughly.
2. Pat the lamb and pork mixture into small burgers. Heat the olive oil in a heavy skillet and add the patties. Cook for 5 minutes per side until they are brown and nicely crusted.
3. Use a fork to break apart the patties and serve over kibble, thinning with more vegetable broth if desired.

Yields 16 servings, serving size 2 tablespoons

1 organic egg, beaten
¼ pound ground pork
¼ pound ground lamb
2 tablespoons Italian parsley, chopped
1 tablespoon fresh mint, chopped
2 tablespoons pine nuts
½ cup long-grain rice, cooked
2 tablespoons virgin olive oil

Pine Nuts

Covered in a hard shell, pine nuts are actually seeds of the pine cone and are not technically nuts at all. Pine nuts can be pressed to extract pine nut oil, a mild nutty oil that is believed to be an appetite suppressant and have antioxidant qualities.

Chapter 11
Seafood

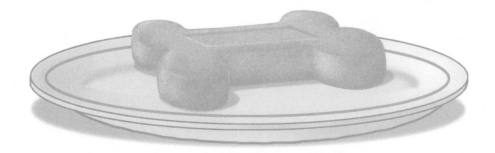

Salmon, Rice, and Broccoli Flash Fry

Canned salmon or any cooked firm-fleshed fish will work for this recipe. Some grocery stores offer a mixed variety of fish cubes for use in seafood stews at a fraction of the cost of purchasing fish fillets.

Yields 16 servings, serving size 2 tablespoons

4 ounces cooked salmon fillet
2 tablespoons virgin olive oil
2 cloves garlic, sliced
½ cup wild rice, cooked
¼ cup frozen chopped broccoli
2 tablespoons organic chicken broth

Salmon Fishing

Popular since ancient times in many coastal areas of the Pacific Northwest, salmon has sustained many cultures for thousands of years. While spearfishing was a popular fishing method, the Ainu peoples of northern Japan employed different tactics. The Ainu taught their dogs to catch salmon as they returned to their breeding grounds en masse.

1. Using a fork, flake the salmon into chunks, carefully removing any bones or skin. Set aside.

2. Heat the olive oil in a heavy saucepan over medium heat. Add the sliced garlic, and then add the rice and broccoli. Using a wooden spoon, keep the broccoli and rice moving in the pan as it cooks. Add the salmon chunks and remove the saucepan from the heat. Add the chicken broth and stir as it sizzles, scraping off any bits that have stuck to the pan.

3. Add more chicken broth if desired and serve over kibble.

Baked Fish Fillets

If you have the time and patience and cut these fillets small enough, they can be served as tasty hors d'oeuvres at your dog's next birthday party. Rather than toothpicks, offer your canine guests unsalted pretzel sticks.

1. Preheat the oven to 350°F.
2. Place the crushed biscuit crumbs on a piece of waxed paper. Dip the fish fillets in the beaten egg and then in the biscuit crumbs. Place the breaded fillets in a baking dish and drizzle with 2 teaspoons olive oil. Cover with foil and bake for 10 minutes. Remove foil and bake an additional 5–10 minutes.
3. Meanwhile, heat the remaining olive oil in a heavy saucepan over medium heat. Add the garlic and broccoli to the oil and sauté. Remove the broccoli from the pan, add some chicken broth to pick up the little bits, and add the mixture to the reserved broccoli.
4. Flake the cooked fish fillets and add them to the sautéed broccoli. Serve over kibble.

Yields 16 servings, serving size 2 tablespoons

½ cup Fish and Chips Biscuits (page 51), crushed
6 ounces whitefish, sliced into small fillets
1 organic egg, beaten
2 tablespoons virgin olive oil
1 clove garlic, chopped
¼ cup frozen chopped broccoli
2 teaspoons organic chicken broth

Biscuit Crumbs

Create your own biscuit crumbs by saving a few biscuits and running them through the food processor. Store the crumbs in a jar or resealable plastic bag in the refrigerator. You can always create a light "gravy" by mixing the biscuit dust with some chicken broth, microwave at high for 20–25 seconds and serve over kibble.

Corn-Stuffed Fish

If your dog can't tolerate corn, you can substitute any vegetable,
including carrots, zucchini, and even beets. For a savory "stuffing,"
add some cooked chicken or turkey sausage meat.

Yields 16 servings, serving size 2 tablespoons

2 tablespoons unbleached
    flour
6 ounces whitefish, sliced into
    small fillets
2 tablespoons virgin olive oil,
    divided
½ cup Fish and Chips
    Biscuits, page 51
¼ cup frozen corn niblets
1 clove garlic, chopped
¼ cup organic chicken broth

1. Preheat the oven to 350°F.
2. Place the flour on a piece of waxed paper. Dip the fish in the flour to coat it. Heat 1 tablespoon olive oil in a heavy saucepan over medium heat. Gently and lightly sauté the floured fillets in the hot oil; remove from the pan to a baking dish. Set aside.
3. Break the biscuits into bite-size bits and mix them with the corn.
4. Add the remaining olive oil to the saucepan. Add the garlic and sauté lightly. Add the biscuits and corn mix and continue to cook 1–2 minutes. Add the chicken broth until the biscuits are softened but not mushy. Spread the corn biscuit mash over the fillets and bake them for 10 minutes.
5. Flake the cooked fish fillets and add extra chicken broth if desired. Serve over kibble.

Maize Maze

The official name for corn is maize, and it's known to grow "as high as an elephant's eye." Mazes of maize are tourist attractions in many farming communities in the United States and Canada. A maze of maize can be designed at the start of a growing season and will mature to the proper height by the start of the summer.

Fish Florentine

Spinach provides twenty-two important nutrients, including vitamins A, K, and C, as well as magnesium, folate, iron, and calcium. Spinach also protects against heart disease, colon cancer, and even arthritis.

1. Preheat the oven to 350°F.
2. Place the flour on a piece of waxed paper. Dip the fish in the flour to coat it. Heat 1 tablespoon olive oil in a heavy saucepan over medium heat. Gently and lightly sauté the floured fillets in the hot oil, and then remove from the pan to a baking dish.
3. Add the remaining olive oil to the saucepan, add the garlic, and sauté it lightly. Add the spinach and continue to cook 1–2 minutes. Remove the spinach from the heat and toss it with the grated cheese. Spread the spinach and cheese mixture on the fillets and bake them for 10 minutes.
4. Flake the cooked fish fillets with the chicken broth and serve over kibble.

Yields 16 servings, serving size 2 tablespoons

2 tablespoons unbleached flour
6 ounces whitefish, sliced into small fillets
2 tablespoons virgin olive oil, divided
1 clove garlic, chopped
¼ cup frozen chopped spinach
2 tablespoons natural Cheddar cheese, grated
2 tablespoons organic chicken broth

Popeye

Still the most famous spinach-eater of all time, Popeye the Sailor was a comic-strip character created by Elzie Crisler Segar. Popeye's popularity helped boost sales of spinach across the country. Alma, Arkansas, which claims to be "The Spinach Capital of the World," and Crystal City, Texas, have both erected statues in Popeye's honor.

Tuna and Vegetable Cakes

There is no need to purchase packaged bread crumbs. You can easily and quickly make your own by running torn bread slices through the food processor. If a recipe calls for dry bread crumbs, toast them in the oven.

Yields 16 servings, serving size 2 tablespoons

1 can chunk white tuna, packed in water
1 slice whole-wheat bread
2 tablespoons Italian flat parsley, chopped
1 organic egg, beaten
½ cup frozen mixed vegetables
2 tablespoons virgin olive oil
2 teaspoons organic chicken broth (optional)

1. Using a fork, finely flake the tuna in a bowl. Tear the bread into pieces and pulse them in a food processor until crumbs form. Fold the bread crumbs, parsley, beaten egg, and mixed vegetables into the tuna.
2. Heat the olive oil in a heavy saucepan over medium heat. While the oil is heating, wet your hand and pat the tuna mixture into small patties. Fry the patties until they are golden brown on both sides.
3. Flake the cooked fish patties with a fork and mix them with the organic chicken broth if desired. Serve over kibble.

Parsley

Parsley is the world's most popular herb and derives its name from the Greek word meaning "rock celery." It has been cultivated for more than 2,000 years and was initially used for medicinal purposes until the Ancient Romans started using it as a garnish. The most common varieties are curly parsley and Italian flat-leaf parsley.

Salmon Croquettes

While very nutritious, salmon has a high fat content, so feed your dog small portions to determine whether she can tolerate it. You can always prepare the croquettes using half salmon and half tuna.

1. Scrub the potatoes, place them in a pot, and cover them with water. Boil them until you can easily pierce the potatoes with a fork, about 25 minutes. Use a fork to mash the potatoes, skin and all, in a bowl.
2. Process the salmon in a food processor so all the bones, cartilage, and skin are finely chopped. Add the salmon to the mashed potatoes. Fold in the parsley, egg, and mixed vegetables.
3. Heat the olive oil in heavy saucepan over medium heat. While the oil is warming, wet your hands and shape the salmon mixture into small patties. Fry the patties until they are golden brown on both sides.
4. Flake the cooked fish patties with the organic chicken broth if desired. Serve over kibble.

Yields 16 servings, serving size 2 tablespoons

3 medium potatoes
1 can salmon, packed in water
2 tablespoons Italian flat parsley, chopped
1 organic egg, beaten
½ cup frozen mixed vegetables
2 tablespoons virgin olive oil
2 teaspoons organic chicken broth

Potatoes

Russets, the most common potato, are high in starch and are ideal for baking, roasting, mashing, and frying. White potatoes are most often thought of as the boiling potato. Red potatoes are perfect for using in salads or roasting, boiling, and steaming. Yellow potatoes have a dense, creamy texture and are great for roasting, baking, boiling, and steaming. Blue and purple potatoes have a subtle nutty flavor.

Tuna Flash-Fry

For convenience, you can purchase shredded carrots at your local market.
If your dog is on a diet or needs to be, carrots are a perfect choice.
Baby carrots that are cleaned and ready to eat are also a perfect option.

Yields 16 servings, serving size 2 tablespoons

1 can chunk white tuna, packed in water
4 teaspoons virgin olive oil, divided
1 clove garlic, chopped
1 carrot, shredded
½ cup frozen peas
2 tablespoons organic chicken broth

Night Vision

Carrots are an excellent source of antioxidant compounds. They are the richest vegetable source of pro-vitamin A carotenes. Their antioxidant compounds help protect the body against cardiovascular disease and cancer and also promote good vision, especially night vision.

1. Using a fork, finely flake the tuna in a bowl. Heat 2 teaspoons olive oil in a heavy saucepan over medium heat. Sauté the garlic until light brown, and then add the carrots. Cook 1–2 minutes and add the peas. Do not overcook.
2. Remove vegetables and heat another 2 teaspoons olive oil. Add the flaked tuna and stir as it sizzles. Leave the tuna on the heat just long enough to heat it through. Remove it from the heat and add the vegetables, stirring till combined.
3. Add the broth and serve over kibble.

White Anchovies and Eggs

The strong taste that people associate with anchovies is due to the curing process. Fresh anchovies, known in Italy as alici, have a much softer and gentler flavor and are sometimes called "white anchovies." You can find them in Italian markets or from a gourmet fishmonger.

1. Heat the olive oil in a heavy saucepan over medium heat. Sauté the garlic till light brown, and then add the anchovy and carrots. Cook for a minute or two, stirring constantly.
2. Pour the beaten eggs into the skillet all at once and scramble with a fork. Cook until the egg is firm.
3. Add the cooked egg mixture to your dog's bowl. Pour in the chicken broth to help cool the mixture and serve over kibble.

Yields 8 servings, serving size ¼ cup

2 teaspoons virgin olive oil
1 clove garlic chopped
1 whole fresh anchovy, chopped
1 carrot, shredded
2 organic eggs, beaten
2 tablespoons organic chicken broth

Anchovies

In Ancient Rome, an anchovy sauce called garum was a popular condiment served with a wide variety of dishes. The sauce consisted of fermented anchovies, eel, and other fishes in a brine of wine, vinegar, pepper, and oil. Pompeii produced a great deal of the Romans' garum. Its production was relegated to the outskirts of the city—in part due to its unpleasant odor.

Puttanesca-Style Sardines

Sardines come packed in tins in a variety of bases, including olive oil, soybean oil, tomato, and even mustard. Look for sardines that are unsalted, boneless, and skinless. Once a tin is open, use the sardines within a week or place them in a resealable plastic bag and freeze them for up to three months.

Yields 8 servings, serving size ¼ cup

2 teaspoons virgin olive oil
2 cloves garlic, chopped
1 skinless, boneless, unsalted sardine, chopped
¼ cup crushed tomatoes
2 tablespoons organic chicken broth

1. Heat the olive oil in a heavy saucepan over medium heat. Sauté the garlic till light brown and then add the chopped sardine. Cook for a minute or two, stirring constantly.
2. Add the crushed tomatoes and chicken broth. Cook at a gentle simmer for 20 minutes. Serve over kibble.

Puttanesca

Traditional puttanesca sauce contains anchovies or sardines, olives, capers, and dried hot pepper flakes. An Italian classic, puttanesca sauce originated in Naples and comes from the Italian slang word *puttana*, meaning prostitute. Since the sauce was quick and inexpensive to prepare, it was a favorite meal for prostitutes to eat between customers.

Sardines and Potato Mash

Sardines and anchovies will "dissolve" if they are cooked too long. If this happens, just continue cooking to reduce the liquid and add a bit more of the potatoes.

1. Cut the sardines into small chunks. Place the flour on a piece of waxed paper and coat the fish with the flour. Set aside.
2. Heat the olive oil in a heavy saucepan over medium heat. Add the garlic and sauté till light brown. Gently and lightly sauté the floured fish chunks in the hot oil; remove them from the pan.
3. Warm the mashed potatoes in the microwave and add the chicken broth, stirring to a smooth consistency. Add the cooked sardines and serve over kibble.

Yields 8 servings, serving size ¼ cup

1 whole skinless, boneless, unsalted sardine
2 tablespoons unbleached flour
1 tablespoon virgin olive oil
2 cloves garlic, chopped
¼ cup mashed potatoes
2 tablespoons organic chicken broth, heated

Chapter 12

Rice and Pasta

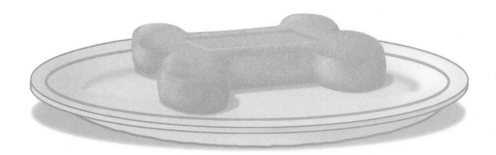

Oven-Baked Rice

This is simply the best and easiest way to prepare rice. It bakes in the oven and comes out light and fluffy every time. If you prefer, you can use chicken broth, vegetable broth, or even water.

Yields 8 servings,
serving size ¼ cup

2 teaspoons virgin olive oil
2 cloves garlic, chopped
1 cup natural brown rice
2 cups organic beef broth
1 tablespoon unsalted butter

1. Preheat the oven to 350°F.
2. Heat the olive oil in a heavy saucepan over medium heat. Add the chopped garlic and sauté until light brown. Add the rice and cook 1–2 minutes until the rice is translucent.
3. Transfer the rice and garlic to an ovenproof casserole dish. Add the beef broth and the butter. Cover the casserole dish.
4. Bake in the oven for 45 minutes or till all the broth is absorbed. Flake the rice with a fork and serve with extra broth over kibble.

Pasta with Olive Oil, Garlic, Zucchini, and Romano Cheese

If you want to recreate the spaghetti scene from Lady and the Tramp, leave the spaghetti at its original length. You could cut your dog's spaghetti, but never, ever put a knife to your own!

1. Bring a heavy pot of water to a rolling boil. Cook the pasta for 7 minutes or until al dente and drain into a colander.
2. While the pasta is cooking, heat the olive oil in a heavy saucepan over medium heat. Add the sliced garlic and sauté till light brown. Add the chopped zucchini and stir constantly with a wooden spoon.
3. Cut the pasta with scissors or a knife and add it to the zucchini mixture. Mix in the grated cheese and serve over kibble.

Yields 8 servings, serving size ¼ cup

6 ounces spaghetti, linguine, or lasagna noodles
2 tablespoons virgin olive oil
4 cloves garlic, sliced
2 small zucchini, finely chopped
3 tablespoons Romano cheese, grated

Selecting Pasta

If you start off using the best-quality ingredients, your final dish will reflect the essence of these flavors. This is most apparent when you compare pasta selection at your grocery store. Imported pasta contains durum wheat semolina, which contains a great deal of starch, protein, and gluten. Less-expensive brands use semolina flour, which is actually a less flavorful white flour that does not hold up when cooked.

Chicken Broth Pastina

Pastina is tiny star-shaped pasta often fed to babies as their first introduction to pasta. You can use pastina in place of rice; the cooking time is much quicker.

Yields 8 servings, serving size ¼ cup

2 teaspoons virgin olive oil
2 cloves garlic, chopped
1 cup pastina
1½ cups organic chicken broth
1 tablespoon Romano cheese, grated

1. Heat the olive oil in a heavy saucepan over medium heat. Add the chopped garlic and sauté until light brown. Add the pastina and cook 1–2 minutes until the pastina is translucent.

2. Add the chicken broth and bring to a boil. Cook at a rolling boil for 4 minutes or till al dente. Do not drain.

3. Flake the pastina with a fork and mix in the grated cheese. Serve over kibble.

Pasta and Sautéed Turkey Sausage

Italian-style sausage should contain only garlic and fennel seed. Do not purchase sausage that is labeled "hot" or contains lots of spices for your dog.

1. Bring a heavy pot of water to a rolling boil. Cook the fusilli for 7 minutes or until al dente and drain in a colander.
2. While the fusilli is cooking, heat the olive oil in a heavy saucepan over medium heat. Add the sliced garlic and sauté till light brown. Remove the casing from the sausage and add the meat to the skillet. Break the sausage meat apart with a wooden spoon and cook until well browned, about 7 minutes. Add the crushed tomatoes and stir till combined. Continue cooking until tomatoes are heated through and sauce thickens slightly.
3. Cut the fusilli with scissors or a knife and add it to the tomato-sausage mixture. Mix in the grated cheese and serve over kibble.

Yields 8 servings, serving size ¼ cup

6 ounces fusilli
1 teaspoon virgin olive oil
4 cloves garlic, sliced
½ cup Italian-style turkey sausage
¼ cup crushed tomatoes
2 tablespoons Romano cheese, grated

Al Dente

The term *al dente* comes from Italian, meaning "to the bite" or "to the tooth" and refers to the ideal doneness of cooked pasta. The most common misnomer is "to the teeth" means that the pasta should stick to the teeth. In actuality, pasta that does stick to your teeth is undercooked. Pasta that is soft, floury, or lacking in texture is overcooked. Perfectly cooked pasta should offer slight resistance and hold its shape.

Pasta and Broccoli

Rigatoni is a tube-shaped pasta that makes perfect-size pasta rings when cut with scissors. You can certainly use fresh broccoli, but the advantage of frozen chopped broccoli is that it will break down, turning into a sauce that really coats the pasta.

Yields 8 servings, serving size ¼ cup

1 cup rigatoni or any tube-shaped pasta
1 tablespoon virgin olive oil
4 cloves garlic, sliced
1 cup frozen broccoli, thawed and finely chopped
2 tablespoons Romano cheese, grated

1. Bring a heavy pot of water to a rolling boil. Cook the pasta for 7 minutes or till al dente and drain into a colander.
2. While the pasta is cooking, heat the olive oil in a heavy saucepan over medium heat. Add the sliced garlic and sauté till light brown. Add the broccoli and stir constantly with a wooden spoon until heated through.
3. Cut the pasta with scissors or a knife, and add to broccoli mixture. Mix in the grated cheese and serve over kibble.

Risotto and Spinach Cakes

Risotto is made from Arborio rice. Cooking risotto correctly requires constant attention and perfect heat. Rather than cooking the rice in liquid that has been added all at once, hot broth is added a little at a time. Wait until the rice absorbs the broth before adding more.

1. Heat 2 teaspoons olive oil in a heavy saucepan over medium heat. Add the sliced garlic and Arborio rice, and sauté until the garlic is light brown and the rice is translucent.
2. Heat the chicken broth in another saucepan. Add ⅓ cup hot chicken broth to the rice and stir constantly with a wooden spoon. Keep adding chicken broth and do not add more until the rice absorbs it. If you run out of chicken broth, add water. The whole process should take about 20 minutes, and the goal is to have rice that is firm but not crunchy and definitely not chalky. If all else fails, you can cook as you would regular long-grain rice, just don't tell anyone.
3. Cool the rice in the refrigerator.
4. Add the chopped spinach, grated cheese, and beaten egg to the cold risotto. Mix thoroughly and form into small patties. Coat the bottom of a skillet with olive oil. Heat the oil. Carefully add the spinach-risotto cakes and fry them until they are browned and crunchy. Break apart with a fork and serve over kibble with extra chicken broth if desired.

Yields 8 servings, serving size ¼ cup

2 teaspoons virgin olive oil, plus a little extra
2 cloves garlic, finely chopped
1 cup Arborio rice
2–3 cups organic chicken broth, plus 2 tablespoons
½ cup frozen chopped spinach, defrosted and squeezed dry
2 tablespoons Romano cheese, grated
1 organic egg, beaten

Arborio Rice

Grown in the Po Valley in the town of Arborio, Italy, Arborio rice is a medium-grain rice that is creamy yet firm when cooked correctly. It is Italian comfort food at its finest and can be used as a base for many recipes. Popular additions are asparagus, artichokes, shrimp, and peas.

Egg Noodles Carbonara

In this recipe, the heat of the noodles actually cooks the raw egg. Thus, all your ingredients must be assembled and ready to go as soon as the noodles are cooked.

Yields 8 cups, serving size ¼ cup

1 organic egg, beaten
2 tablespoons Romano cheese, grated
1 piece Applegate Farms Sunday bacon, cooked and crumbled
6 ounces egg noodles
2 teaspoons virgin olive oil
2 cloves garlic, sliced
organic chicken broth (optional)

1. Place an empty glass measuring cup in the microwave and heat it for 20 seconds on high power. Carefully remove the measuring cup and add the egg, grated cheese, and crumbled bacon. Use a fork or whisk to completely emulsify the egg. Set the mixture aside.

2. Bring a heavy pot of water to a rolling boil. Cook the egg noodles for 5 minutes or till al dente. Save some pasta water in a measuring cup.

3. While the pasta is cooking, heat the olive oil in a small saucepan over medium heat. Add the sliced garlic and sauté till light brown. When the noodles are ready, drain them in a colander and quickly return them to the hot pasta pot. Toss the cooked noodles with the olive oil and garlic mixture.

4. Add about 1 tablespoon pasta water to the egg mixture and pour it all at once onto the noodles. Mix thoroughly and carefully with a wooden spoon. Use two knives to cut the pasta in a crisscross fashion. Serve over kibble with chicken broth if desired.

Anchovy Baked Ziti

The uncooked pasta will absorb the tomato sauce as it bakes in the oven, and you will end up with pasta that is al dente and not overcooked.

1. Preheat oven to 350°F. Heat the olive oil in a small saucepan over medium heat. Add the sliced garlic and sauté until light brown.
2. Place the uncooked ziti in a small casserole dish; toss the ziti with the olive oil and garlic mixture.
3. Mix the spinach and ¼ cup chicken broth, and add to the Anchovy Tomato Sauce. Add this mixture to the pasta and toss until the pasta is coated with the sauce.
3. Cover the casserole dish with a piece of foil; use a sharp knife to make several slits in the foil to act as steam vents. Bake for 30 minutes and remove the foil. Bake another 5–10 minutes or till a nice crust has formed.
4. Use two knives to cut the pasta in a crisscross fashion. Serve over kibble with chicken broth if desired.

Yields 8 servings, serving size ¼ cup

2 teaspoons virgin olive oil
2 cloves garlic, sliced
6 ounces ziti
½ cup frozen spinach, thawed and squeezed dry
¼ cup organic chicken broth, plus a little extra
½ cup Tomato, Anchovy, and Rice Soup, page 204, made without the rice

Using Uncooked Pasta

Lasagna and macaroni and cheese are two other pasta dishes that don't require cooked noodles. Baking raw noodles with other ingredients results in pasta that is not overcooked or mushy. Between the moisture of the sauce and the steam from being covered, the uncooked pasta has plenty of time to cook. This trick also speeds up the preparation process.

Orzo Macaroni and Cheese

Orzo is a seed-shaped pasta that cooks quickly and is the perfect-size pasta for any dog. You can use orzo in any recipe that calls for rice if you prefer.

Yields 8 servings,
serving size ¼ cup

2 teaspoons virgin olive oil
2 cloves garlic, chopped
1 cup orzo
1 cup organic chicken broth
1 tablespoon Romano cheese,
*   grated*
1 tablespoon natural sharp
*   Cheddar cheese, grated*
1 tablespoon fresh bread
*   crumbs*

1. Preheat the oven to 400°F.
2. Heat the olive oil in a heavy saucepan over medium heat. Add the chopped garlic and sauté until light brown. Add the orzo and cook 1–2 minutes until the orzo is translucent.
3. Add the chicken broth and bring to a boil. Cook at a rolling boil for 4 minutes or till al dente. Do not drain.
4. Pour the orzo and broth into a casserole dish and use a fork to mix in the grated cheeses. Sprinkle the bread crumbs on top, drizzle with a little olive oil, and place the dish in the oven for 5 minutes or until the bread crumbs are toasted and browned nicely.

Pesto Wild Rice with Grilled Chicken and Pears

The pears add a delicate sweetness and crunch that complements the pesto perfectly. When buying pesto, be sure to select fresh pesto that does not contain preservatives. You should use fresh pesto within a week of purchasing, but you can always freeze the extra.

1. Heat 2 teaspoons olive oil in a heavy saucepan over medium heat. Add the chopped garlic and sauté until light brown. Add the rice and cook 1–2 minutes until the rice is translucent.
2. Add the chicken broth and bring to a boil. Cook, covered, at a very low simmer for 30 minutes or till chicken broth is absorbed.
3. While the rice is cooking, heat a grill pan over medium heat. Toss the sliced chicken breast in the remaining olive oil and place it on the hot grill. Do not turn the pieces until the chicken has grill marks and no longer sticks to the pan. If the chicken sticks, allow it to cook 1 minute longer.
4. When the chicken is cool enough to handle, shred it into bite-size pieces.
5. Stir the pesto and the chopped pears into the cooked rice. Add the shredded grilled chicken and toss till just combined. Flake the rice with a fork and serve over kibble, with extra chicken broth if desired.

Yields 8 servings, serving size ¼ cup

4 teaspoons virgin olive oil, separated
2 cloves garlic, chopped
1 cup wild rice
2 cups organic chicken broth, plus a little extra
1 chicken breast, cut into thick slices
1 tablespoon pesto
1 pear, peeled and finely chopped

Pears

A visit to a farmers' market will allow you to sample pears and compare taste, texture, skin thickness, and feel. Bartlett pears are sweet and juicy; they are often used for canning or cooking. Anjou pears are green or red and retain their color when ripe. Bosc pears' dense flesh makes them an ideal choice for cooking and baking.

Couscous with Tomato and Pine Nuts

Couscous is available in a variety of flavors. Select a spinach, tomato, or vegetable-blend variety for added kick. Couscous will clump when refrigerated, but you can easily crumble it with your fingers and reheat it with chicken broth or water.

Yields 2 servings,
serving size ½ cup

2 cups organic chicken broth,
    plus a little extra
2 teaspoons virgin olive oil
2 cloves garlic, chopped
1 cup vegetable-flavored
    couscous
1 tablespoon Romano cheese,
    grated
2 tablespoons canned
    chopped tomatoes
1 tablespoon pine nuts,
    lightly toasted

1. Pour the chicken broth into a saucepan and bring to a boil. While the broth is heating, add the olive oil to a saucepan along with the chopped garlic and sauté until light brown. Add the couscous, and cook 1–2 minutes until translucent.

2. Pour the boiling chicken broth over the couscous, cover, and let sit for 5 minutes. Flake with a fork and gently stir in the grated cheese, chopped tomatoes, and toasted pine nuts.

3. Serve over kibble with extra chicken broth if desired.

Couscous

Couscous is a coarsely ground semolina pasta that is a staple in many North African countries. Couscous is traditionally served under a meat or vegetable stew. Commercially packaged couscous has been steamed and dried, so the addition of boiling water or broth cooks the couscous almost immediately.

Sushi Rice with Dried Anchovies and Shredded Nori

This recipe is an ode to Japanese-style cuisine. It combines commonly used
ingredients that are highly nutritious and packed with vitamins and minerals.

1. Heat the olive oil in a heavy saucepan over medium heat. Add the chopped garlic and sauté till light brown. Add the rice and cook 1–2 minutes until the rice is translucent.
2. Add 2 cups chicken broth and bring to a boil. Cover and cook at a very low simmer for 30 minutes or till chicken broth is absorbed.
3. While the rice is cooking, crumble the dried anchovies into the remaining tablespoon of chicken broth. Microwave for 23 seconds; stir to break up and dissolve the dried anchovies. Set aside.
4. Using a very sharp knife, cut the nori into fine slivers to resemble confetti. Set aside.
5. When the rice is cooked, add the anchovy chicken broth and stir until combined. Flake the rice with a fork and toss with kibble, adding extra chicken broth if desired. Sprinkle 2 teaspoons of the finely chopped nori over each portion and stir once more before serving.

Yields 8 servings, serving size ¼ cup

2 teaspoons virgin olive oil
2 cloves garlic, chopped
1 cup sushi rice
2 cups plus 1 tablespoon organic chicken broth
1 tablespoon unsalted dried anchovies, crumbled
2 tablespoons nori

Nori

Nori is the Japanese name for edible seaweed that has been dried and processed into sheets. Nori is used in sushi rolls and can also be eaten on its own or crumbled on top of rice, salads, and entrées. Available in sheets and shredded flakes, nori is rich in calcium, zinc, and iodine. Nori is naturally salty and should be eaten in limited amounts by individuals on a restricted salt diet.

Chapter 13
Let's Have a Party!

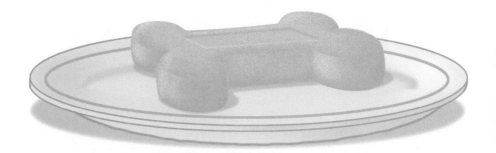

Oatmeal Cheese Straws

You can prepare the dough ahead of time, but it's best to bake these cheese straws the same day you plan to serve them. If you must make them in advance, crisp them in a warm oven before serving.

Yields 30 straws

¼ cup sweet Italian sausage, cooked and crumbled

1 cup natural Cheddar cheese, grated

¼ cup Romano cheese, grated

1 cup oat flour

1½ cups old-fashioned rolled oats

¼ cup canola oil

3 tablespoons organic chicken broth

1. Combine the crumbled sausage and grated cheeses in a mixing bowl. Add the flour and rolled oats; mix until combined.
2. Combine the canola oil and chicken broth in a glass measuring cup and pour all at once into the cheese-flour mixture. Stir until it forms a soft dough. Shape into a disc, wrap in plastic wrap, and refrigerate for 2 hours.
3. Heat the oven to 400°F. Remove the dough from the refrigerator and tear off small pieces. Roll the pieces between your palms to create ropes. Hold both ends of each rope and twist it into a spiral. Press the ends of each spiral onto a cookie sheet lined with parchment paper. Bake for 7 minutes till nicely browned and crunchy.

Mini–Italian Sweet Sausage Heroes

Purchase the Italian bread from an Italian bakery or a good gourmet grocery store that bakes it fresh daily. Good Italian bread has a hard and crunchy crust that toasts beautifully and tastes wonderful.

1. Remove sausage from the casing and use your hands to mix the sausage and ground lamb with the beaten egg and minced garlic. Add the rolled oats and grated cheese. Wet your hands and form the mixture into small rectangular-shaped patties, about 2 by 3 inches.
2. Heat the grill pan over medium heat. Lightly spray it with nonstick spray. Grill the patties 7 minutes each side.
3. Slice each bread section in half and place it on the grill. Toast the bread lightly. When the patties are cool enough, place them on the bread and serve.

Yield 16 servings, serving size 2 tablespoons

4 ounces sweet Italian sausage
4 ounces ground lamb
1 organic egg, beaten
1 clove garlic, minced
4 tablespoons old-fashioned rolled oats
2 tablespoons Romano cheese, grated
1 loaf Italian bread, cut into 3-inch sections

Tricky to Eat

These Italian heroes will look great on your buffet table, but your smaller guests might have a tough time eating the bread and meat as a sandwich. Be sure to have a bread knife available to cut into appropriately sized bites. You can even remove some of the soft bread on the inside of each loaf and flatten the whole loaf with a rolling pin.

Chicken Pops

These chicken pops are perfect for a hot day and are best enjoyed outside. You can form the pops in small paper cups, but if you have access to bone-shaped ice-cube trays, your guests—both two-legged and four-legged—will be thrilled.

Yields 3 cups

2 cups organic chicken broth
2 cups filtered water
½ cup carrot, grated
½ cup green apple, finely chopped
small paper cups or fancy-shaped ice-cube trays

Ice Pop Variations
You can alter the flavor of the pops by using beef broth or even vegetable broth. Add cubes of cooked meat and assorted vegetables such as peas, broccoli, and spinach for fun flavors. You can also combine blueberries and beets for a colorful and tasty pop.

1. Combine the chicken broth, water, carrots, and apple in a glass measuring cup and mix until combined.
2. Place the measuring cup in the freezer for 2 hours. Check the contents of the bowl, mixing the slush with a fork to distribute the carrot and apple throughout.
3. Before the broth mixture is frozen, transfer desired amounts to the small paper cups or ice-cube trays. Return to the freezer and freeze overnight or till solid.
4. To serve, remove the paper cup or pop from the ice-cube tray and place it on the grass next to your dog.

Cranberry Coconut Granola

You can use scissors to cut the cranberries; an ulu knife and a cutting board will also work. Ulu knives have a sharp crescent-shaped blade that is perfect for chopping small ingredients.

1. Preheat the oven to 350°F.
2. Place the oats, coconut, cranberries, and cinnamon in a mixing bowl and whisk until combined.
3. Combine the peanut butter and rice syrup in a glass measuring cup and stir it with a fork until the mixture is smooth and creamy.
4. Add the peanut butter mixture to the oat mixture and mix them on a medium speed using a paddle attachment until they are combined. The mixture will be sticky.
5. Press the oat mixture into a parchment-lined jelly-roll pan. Bake 12–15 minutes until it is golden and crispy. Allow to cool and use a knife to cut it into small bars or break into bits.

Yields 30 bars

2½ cups old-fashioned rolled oats
½ cup unsweetened flaked coconut
½ cup unsweetened dried cranberries, chopped
1 teaspoon cinnamon
½ cup unsalted natural crunchy peanut butter
½ cup organic brown rice syrup

Ulu Knives
Ulu knives were created by the Inuit people as a hunting and cooking tool. They have a long curved blade and a handle designed to fit comfortably in the palm of the hand. They can be rocked back and forth over ingredients to chop them into small pieces. They resemble a single-bladed mezzaluna with one handle. Ulu can be purchased online from specialty retailers.

Mini–Chicken Pot Pies

Try filling the phyllo shells with BBQ Beef Stew on page 126, or Chicken Stew on page 115. Any cooked or thickened filling can be used successfully.

. . . .

Yields 15 minitarts

1 box mini–phyllo dough shells, defrosted
1 cup long-grain rice, cooked
2 tablespoons organic chicken broth
3 tablespoons natural Cheddar cheese, grated
1 cup cooked chicken breast, chopped
½ cup frozen peas and carrots, thawed

1. Preheat the oven to 350°F. Place the defrosted phyllo shells on a cookie sheet and bake them in the oven for 5 minutes or until crisp.
2. Use a fork to mix the rice with the chicken broth, 2 tablespoons grated cheese, chicken, and peas and carrots. Fill the tart shells with the rice and chicken mixture. Sprinkle them with the remaining cheese and bake the pies in the oven for 10 minutes or until the cheese is melted and browned nicely.

Carob–Peanut Butter Cups

You can find candy molds in assorted shapes at specialty stores.
Fun shapes include shoe soles, paw prints, and detailed hearts.

1. Process the Peanut Butter–Spice Biscuits in a food processor until they turn into crumbs.
2. Place the biscuit crumbs, oats, carob, and cinnamon in a mixing bowl and whisk until combined.
3. Combine the peanut butter and organic brown rice syrup in a glass measuring cup and stir with a fork until smooth and creamy.
4. Add the peanut butter mixture to the crumb mixture and mix on medium speed using a paddle attachment until combined. The mixture will be sticky.
5. Wet your hands and shape the batter into small balls or press it into the desired molds. Store the treats in a tin in the refrigerator for up to 1 month.

Yields 30 bars

2½ cups Peanut Butter–Spice Biscuits, page 48
½ cup old-fashioned rolled oats
1 tablespoon unsweetened carob powder
½ teaspoon cinnamon
¼ cup unsalted natural smooth peanut butter
½ cup organic brown rice syrup

Make It Fancy

You can create carob icing by mixing carob powder with canola oil until it is smooth and shiny. Drizzle the icing over "sweet" treats like biscotti, granola bars, and rolled biscuits that contain carob, peanut butter, or fruit. Use the icing sparingly; while it looks sweet, it won't offer flavor unless you add a teaspoon of pure vanilla and even a pinch of cinnamon.

Pasta, Peas, and Pancetta

Pancetta is available in Italian delis and in the meat departments of select grocery stores. Pancetta is Italian bacon. It adds a distinctive flavor to everything. Cut into fine bits when cooking; a little pancetta goes a long way.

Yields 8 servings,
serving size ¼ cup

6 ounces penne
1 teaspoon virgin olive oil
2 cloves garlic, sliced
1 ounce pancetta
¼ cup frozen peas, defrosted
½ cup organic chicken broth
2 tablespoons Romano
*   cheese, grated*

1. Bring a heavy pot of water to a rolling boil. Do not add salt to the water. Cook the pasta for 7 minutes or till al dente and drain in a colander.
2. While the pasta is cooking, heat the olive oil in a heavy saucepan over medium heat. Add the sliced garlic and sauté until light brown. Finely chop the pancetta and add it to the skillet. Cook the pancetta until it is well browned, about 3 minutes. Add the peas and chicken broth, stirring until combined and heated through.
3. Cut the pasta with scissors or a knife and add it to the broth mixture. Mix in the grated cheese and serve it over kibble.

Risotto Cakes with Peas and Broccoli

Use a wide, flat spoon to shape the risotto cakes. Press the rice mixture into the spoon and gently slide each cake into the hot oil. Use a fry screen to prevent the hot oil from "spitting," which can burn your skin and splatter your stovetop.

1. Heat 2 teaspoons olive oil in a heavy saucepan over medium heat. Add the sliced garlic and rice; sauté them until the garlic is light brown and the rice is translucent.
2. Heat the chicken broth in another saucepan. Add ⅓ cup of the hot chicken broth to the rice and stir constantly with a wooden spoon. Keep adding the chicken broth, but do not add more until the rice absorbs it. If you run out of chicken broth, add water. The whole process should take about 20 minutes, and the goal is to have rice that is firm but not crunchy and definitely not chalky.
3. Cool the rice in the refrigerator before proceeding with the recipe.
4. Add the peas, broccoli, grated cheese, and egg to the cold risotto. Mix thoroughly and form into small patties. Heat the remaining oil; there should be enough to cover the bottom of the skillet. Carefully add the risotto cakes and fry them 5 minutes a side until they are browned and crunchy. Serve over kibble with extra chicken broth if desired.

Yields 8 servings, serving size ¼ cup

2 teaspoons plus 1 teaspoon virgin olive oil
2 cloves garlic, finely chopped
1 cup Arborio rice
3–4 cups organic chicken broth
½ cup frozen peas, defrosted
¼ cup frozen chopped broccoli, defrosted
2 tablespoons Romano cheese, grated
1 organic egg, beaten

Resistance is Futile

To prevent the cakes from breaking apart during the frying process, resist the temptation to turn them before they are ready. The cakes need to cook a solid 5 minutes per side, and they will have a nicely browned crust when they are ready to flip.

Chicken Satay

Be sure to have your guests remove the chicken from the skewers before they give them to their dog. The bamboo skewers can splinter if dogs chew on them.

Yields 8 servings,
serving size ¼ cup

*2 tablespoons organic
   chicken broth
2 tablespoons unsalted
   natural peanut butter
1 chicken breast, cut into
   thick slices
2 teaspoons virgin olive oil
6 bamboo skewers*

1. Combine the chicken broth and peanut butter in a glass measuring cup. Using a whisk, stir until the mixture is smooth.
2. Heat the grill pan over medium heat. Toss the sliced chicken breast in the olive oil, and thread 2 to 3 chicken pieces onto each skewer. Place skewers onto the hot grill. Do not turn until the chicken has grill marks and no longer sticks to the pan. If the chicken sticks, allow it to cook a minute longer.
3. Remove the grilled chicken and use a silicone pastry brush to lightly coat the chicken with the peanut butter mixture. Return to the grill for another minute or until the peanut butter is set and slightly browned.

Pigs 'n Blankets

You can prep the pigs 'n blankets and keep them frozen until you are ready to bake them. Store the unbaked pigs in a resealable plastic bag for up to 2 months.

1. Combine the grated cheeses, oat flour, and rolled oats in a mixing bowl and mix until combined.
2. Pour the canola oil and chicken broth into a glass measuring cup and then all at once into the bowl. Stir until a soft dough forms; shape the dough into a disc. Wrap it in plastic wrap and refrigerate for 2 hours.
3. Heat the oven to 400°F. Roll the dough ¼-inch thick into a rectangle that is 6 inches wide. Place a whole hot dog on the dough and roll it up to completely cover the hot dog. Moisten the dough with water to seal the dough around the hot dog.
4. Place the hot dogs in the freezer for 30 minutes. Remove the slightly frozen hot dogs and slice them into ½-inch segments. Place the cut pieces on a parchment-lined cookie sheet and bake for 7 minutes until nicely browned.

Yields 45 mini pigs 'n blankets

½ cup natural Cheddar cheese, grated
¼ cup Romano cheese, grated
1 cup oat flour
1½ cups old-fashioned rolled oats
¼ cup canola oil
3 tablespoons organic chicken broth
4 organic beef or chicken hot dogs

Helpful Hint

To keep foods from sticking, place individual pieces on a parchment-lined cookie sheet and place it in the freezer for 15 minutes. The partially frozen pieces will no longer stick together even when placed in a resealable plastic bag. You can use this storage method for everything from hamburgers to cut-out biscuits and pigs 'n blankets.

Chapter 14

Celebration Cakes

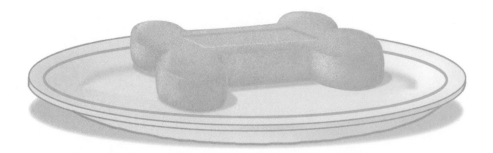

Carrot Cake with Turkey Sausage Crumbles

Carrot cake is a healthy and tasty choice for any celebration. Be sure to put less cream frosting on than you would if you made the cake for yourself.

. . . .

Yields 1 double-layered
8-inch cake

1 cup canola oil
4 organic eggs
2 cups unbleached flour
2 teaspoons baking soda
1 teaspoon cinnamon
3½ cups carrots, shredded
½ cup turkey sausage, cooked
1 recipe Cream Cheese
    Frosting (following the
    recipe on page 181)

1. Preheat the oven to 350°F. Grease and flour two 8-inch cake pans.
2. In a mixing bowl, cream the canola oil and brown rice syrup at medium speed. Add eggs one at a time, beating after each one is added.
3. Sift the flour, baking soda, and cinnamon onto a piece of waxed paper. Add the sifted dry ingredients to the mixing bowl, and beat until mixed. Fold in the shredded carrots and turkey sausage.
4. Divide the batter between the cake pans. Bake for 30 minutes or until a cake tester comes out clean. Allow the cake to cool in the pans for 10 minutes before removing the pans and transferring the cake onto a cooling rack.
5. Allow the cake layers to cool completely before frosting. Frost with the cream cheese frosting.

Cream Cheese Frosting

Cream the softened cream cheese in a mixer until smooth. Add the milk and vanilla. Beat the mixture until it is smooth and creamy. Using an offset spatula, frost the cake layers with a thin layer of cream cheese frosting. Refrigerate the cake for 20 minutes before applying a second layer of frosting.

1 8-ounce package cream cheese, softened
¼ cup milk
2 teaspoons pure vanilla

Banana Carob Chip

For individual portions, you can bake minicupcakes without any liners. To frost, simply hold the cupcake by the base, plunge the top into the frosting, pull it up, and twist it as if it were a soft-serve ice-cream cone.

Yields 1 double-layered 8-inch cake

1 cup canola oil
4 organic eggs
2 cups unbleached flour
2 teaspoons baking soda
1 teaspoon cinnamon
2 ripe bananas, mashed
¼ cup unsweetened carob chips, chopped
1 recipe Cream Cheese Frosting, page 181

Tough Chopping

Use a food processor to chop tough items such as carob chips, but add small amounts of the ingredient at a time. If you don't like the "dust" this creates, simply pour the contents into a wire mesh strainer and shake them off over the sink.

1. Preheat the oven to 350°F. Grease and flour two 8-inch cake pans.
2. In a mixing bowl, cream the canola oil and brown rice syrup at medium speed. Add the eggs one at a time, beating after each one is added.
3. Sift the flour, baking soda, and cinnamon onto a piece of waxed paper. Add the sifted ingredients to the egg-oil mixture, and beat until they are thoroughly combined. Fold in the bananas and carob chips.
4. Divide the batter between the two cake pans. Bake for 30 minutes or until the cake tester comes out clean. Allow the cake to cool in the pans for 10 minutes before removing the pans and transferring the cake to a cooling rack.
5. Allow the cake layers to cool completely before frosting them. Frost with Cream Cheese Frosting.

Peanut Butter and Banana

Since peanut butter is a "heavy" ingredient, be sure to mix it thoroughly with the other wet ingredients before adding any of the dry ingredients.

. . . .

1. Preheat the oven to 350°F. Grease and flour two 8-inch cake pans.
2. In a mixing bowl, cream the canola oil and brown rice syrup at medium speed. Add the peanut butter and beat well. Add eggs one at a time, beating after each one is added.
3. Sift the flour, baking soda, and cinnamon onto a piece of waxed paper. Add the sifted ingredients to the egg-oil mixture and beat until combined. Fold in the mashed banana.
4. Divide the batter between the cake pans. Bake for 30 minutes or until the cake tester comes out clean. Allow the cake to cool in the pans for 10 minutes before removing the pans and transferring the cake onto a cooling rack.
5. Allow the cake layers to cool completely before frosting. Frost with Cream Cheese Frosting.

Yields 1 double-layered 8-inch cake

1 cup canola oil
¼ cup natural peanut butter
4 organic eggs
2 cups unbleached flour
2 teaspoons baking soda
1 teaspoon cinnamon
2 bananas, mashed
1 recipe Cream Cheese
   Frosting, page 181

Preparing Cake Pans

It is essential that you grease and flour cake pans to avoid a cake sticking to the pan. For the "grease," you can use a cooking spray, canola oil, or even shortening. Do not use butter; it will burn and smoke. Add the flour to the pan and tap it with the heel of your hand to distribute it evenly to the bottom and sides of the pan.

Pumpkin Spice

You can use the leftover pumpkin from this recipe to bake the Pumpkin Pie Biscuits, page 39. You can also substitute it with cooked sweet potato with very good results.

Yields 1 double-layered 8-inch cake

1 cup canola oil
½ cup organic brown rice syrup, if desired
4 organic eggs
½ cup pumpkin purée
1 teaspoon pure vanilla
2 cups unbleached flour
2 teaspoons baking soda
2 teaspoons cinnamon
1 teaspoon ground ginger
1 recipe Cream Cheese Frosting, page 181

1. Preheat the oven to 350°F. Grease and flour two 8-inch cake pans.
2. In a mixing bowl, cream the canola oil and brown rice syrup at medium speed. Add the eggs one at a time, beating after each addition. Add the pumpkin purée and vanilla.
3. Sift the flour, baking soda, cinnamon, and ginger onto a piece of waxed paper. Add the sifted ingredients to the egg-oil mixture and beat until combined.
4. Divide the batter between the cake pans. Bake for 30 minutes or until a cake tester comes out clean. Allow the cake to cool in pans for 10 minutes before removing the pans and transferring cake onto a cooling rack.
5. Allow the cake layers to cool completely before frosting. Frost with Cream Cheese Frosting.

Blueberry Banana Almond

You can certainly use fresh blueberries for this recipe, but the frozen ones defrost into a slightly mushy and pulpy consistency that is perfect for cakes. For blueberry pie, always use fresh blueberries.

1. Preheat the oven to 350°F. Grease and flour two 8-inch cake pans.
2. In a mixing bowl, cream the canola oil and brown rice syrup at medium speed. Add the eggs one at a time, beating after each addition. Add the thawed blueberries.
3. Sift the flour, baking soda, and cinnamon onto a piece of waxed paper. Add the sifted ingredients to the egg-oil mixture and beat until combined. Fold in the mashed bananas and chopped almonds.
4. Divide the batter between the cake pans. Bake for 30 minutes or until a cake tester comes out clean. Allow the cake to cool in pans for 10 minutes before removing the pans and transferring the cake onto a cooling rack.
5. Allow the cake layers to cool completely before frosting. Frost with Cream Cheese Frosting.

Yields 1 double-layered 8-inch cake

1 cup canola oil
4 organic eggs
½ cup frozen blueberries, thawed
2 cups unbleached flour
2 teaspoons baking soda
2 teaspoons cinnamon
2 bananas, mashed
¼ cup almonds, finely chopped
1 recipe Cream Cheese Frosting, page 181

Paper Cake Pans

If you are taking your cake to the park for a birthday celebration, you might consider baking it in a paper cake pan. Available at specialty cooking stores, the pans are imported from Italy and France. Decorative, sturdy, and inexpensive, they make for an easy presentation and are available in many shapes and sizes.

Rice Cake

This cake is a sort of rice pudding in the form of a cake.
If you are tempted to add raisins, don't. They can be toxic to your dog.

Yields 1 double-layered
8-inch cake

1 cup canola oil
1 cup brown rice, cooked
¼ cup sour cream
4 organic eggs
2 cups unbleached flour
2 teaspoons baking soda
2 teaspoons cinnamon
½ cup apple, finely chopped
1 recipe Cream Cheese
    Frosting, page 181

1. Preheat oven to 350°F. Grease and flour two 8-inch cake pans.
2. In a mixing bowl, cream the canola oil, brown rice, and sour cream at medium speed. Add eggs one at a time, beating after each addition.
3. Sift the flour, baking soda, and cinnamon onto a piece of waxed paper. Add the sifted ingredients to egg-oil mixture and beat until combined. Fold in the chopped apples.
4. Divide the batter between the cake pans. Bake for 30 minutes or until a cake tester comes out clean. Allow the cake to cool in the pans for 10 minutes before removing the pans and transferring the cake to a cooling rack.
5. Allow the cake layers to cool completely before frosting. Frost with Cream Cheese Frosting.

Applesauce Cake

*If you go apple picking in the fall, remember to save
a few to make treats for your dog!*

1. Preheat the oven to 350°F. Grease and flour two 8-inch cake pans.
2. In a mixing bowl, cream the canola oil, applesauce, and sour cream at medium speed. Add the eggs one at a time, beating after each addition.
3. Sift the flour, baking soda, and cinnamon onto a piece of waxed paper. Add the sifted ingredients to the egg-oil mixture and beat until combined. Fold in the chopped apples.
4. Divide the batter between the cake pans. Bake for 30 minutes or until a cake tester comes out clean. Allow the cake to cool in the pans for 10 minutes before removing the pans and transferring the cake to a cooling rack.
5. Allow the cake layers to cool completely before frosting. Frost with Cream Cheese Frosting.

Yields 1 double-layered
8-inch cake

½ cup canola oil
½ cup organic unsweetened
    applesauce
¼ cup sour cream
4 organic eggs
2 cups unbleached flour
2 teaspoons baking soda
2 teaspoons cinnamon
½ cup apple, finely chopped
1 recipe Cream Cheese
    Frosting, page 181

Unsweetened Applesauce

Unsweetened applesauce is sometimes difficult to find. Make your own by combining chopped apples, water, and a cinnamon stick in a pot and cooking until the apples are soft. Remove the cinnamon stick and process the mixture in the food processor until creamy and smooth.

Spinach and Bacon

Savory cakes are the best option you can offer your dog and her friends.
They work for either a morning or afternoon celebration.

. . . .

Yields 1 double-layered
8-inch cake

½ cup canola oil
½ cup frozen chopped
   spinach, thawed and
   squeezed dry
¼ cup sour cream
4 organic eggs
2 cups unbleached flour
2 teaspoons baking soda
2 pieces Applegate Farms
   Sunday bacon, cooked
   and crumbled
½ cup apple, finely chopped
1 recipe Cream Cheese
   Frosting, page 181

1. Preheat the oven to 350°F. Grease and flour two 8-inch cake pans.

2. In a mixing bowl, cream the canola oil, spinach, and sour cream at medium speed. Add the eggs one at a time, beating after each addition.

3. Sift the flour and baking soda onto a piece of waxed paper. Add the sifted ingredients to the egg-oil mixture and beat until combined. Fold in the crumbled bacon and chopped apples.

4. Divide the batter between the cake pans. Bake for 30 minutes or until a cake tester comes out clean. Allow the cake to cool in the pans for 10 minutes before removing pans and transferring the cake to a cooling rack.

5. Allow the cake layers to cool completely before frosting. Frost with Cream Cheese Frosting.

Liver and Peas

Open the window when you bake this cake; the liver smell is a bit strong and not to everyone's liking. Plan to do all your liver cooking in one day.

1. Preheat the oven to 350°F. Grease and flour two 8-inch cake pans.
2. In a mixing bowl, cream the canola oil, cooked liver, and sour cream at medium speed. Add the eggs one at a time, beating after each addition.
3. Sift the flour and baking soda onto a piece of waxed paper. Add the sifted ingredients to the egg-oil mixture and beat until combined. Fold in the crumbled bacon and peas.
4. Divide the batter between the cake pans. Bake for 30 minutes or until a cake tester comes out clean. Allow the cake to cool in the pans for 10 minutes before removing the pans and transferring the cake to a cooling rack.
5. Allow the cake layers to cool completely before frosting. Frost with Cream Cheese Frosting.

Yields 1 double-layered 8-inch cake

½ cup canola oil
¼ cup cooked liver
¼ cup sour cream
4 organic eggs
2 cups unbleached flour
2 teaspoons baking soda
1 piece Applegate Farms Sunday bacon, cooked and crumbled
½ cup frozen peas, thawed
1 recipe Cream Cheese Frosting, page 181

Decorating with Peas

You can use peas as you would chopped nuts, and apply them to the sides and top of a frosted cake for a quick and healthy decoration. Be sure the peas are defrosted and patted dry. Use a gentle hand when applying the peas; do not press them too far into the frosting. You will need an extra bag to completely cover a double-layered cake.

Peanut Butter and Bacon

Peanut butter and bacon are a great combination and make a very decadent sandwich. You can substitute banana, sweet potato, carrots, or even pumpkin for the apple in this recipe.

Yields 1 double-layered
8-inch cake

1 cup canola oil
¼ cup natural peanut butter
4 organic eggs
2 cups unbleached flour
2 teaspoons baking soda
2 pieces Applegate Farms Sunday bacon, cooked and crumbled
½ cup apple, finely chopped
1 recipe Cream Cheese Frosting, page 181

1. Preheat the oven to 350°F. Grease and flour two 8-inch cake pans.
2. In a mixing bowl, cream the canola oil and peanut butter at medium speed. Add the eggs one at a time, beating after each addition.
3. Sift the flour and baking soda onto a piece of waxed paper. Add the sifted ingredients to the egg-oil mixture and beat until combined. Fold in the crumbled bacon and chopped apple.
4. Divide the batter between the cake pans. Bake for 30 minutes or until a cake tester comes out clean. Allow the cake to cool in the pans for 10 minutes before removing the pans and transferring the cake to a cooling rack.
5. Allow the cake layers to cool completely before frosting. Frost with Cream Cheese Frosting.

Black Velvet Cake

Carrots provide additional flavor and texture to this traditional favorite.

1. Preheat the oven to 350°F. Grease and flour two 8-inch cake pans.
2. Process the beets in a food processor until finely chopped. In a mixing bowl, cream the canola oil and beets at medium speed. Add the eggs one at a time, beating after each addition.
3. Sift the flour and baking soda onto a piece of waxed paper. Add the sifted ingredients to the egg-oil mixture and beat until combined. Fold in the shredded carrots and turkey sausage.
4. Divide the batter between the cake pans. Bake for 30 minutes or until a cake tester comes out clean. Allow the cake to cool in the pans for 10 minutes before removing the pans and transferring them to a cooling rack.
5. Allow the cake layers to cool completely before frosting. Frost with Cream Cheese Frosting.

Yields 1 double-layered 8-inch cake

1 cup canned beets, no sugar added
1 cup canola oil
4 organic eggs
2 cups unbleached flour
2 teaspoons baking soda
1 cup carrots, shredded
¼ cup turkey sausage, cooked
1 recipe Cream Cheese Frosting, page 181

Black Velvet Coloring

Traditional black velvet cake uses cocoa and red food coloring to achieve its distinctive deep red color. Here beets are used to create a natural red hue. Cocoa is omitted for obvious reasons.

Carob, Banana, and Dried Cherry

You can make a carob icing by combining carob powder with organic brown rice syrup and whisking thoroughly. Keep the icing thin and drizzle it on cakes, cupcakes, or biscuits.

Yields 1 double-layered
8-inch cake

1 cup canola oil
½ cup organic brown rice syrup, if desired
4 organic eggs
2 cups unbleached flour
¼ cup carob powder
2 teaspoons baking soda
1 teaspoon cinnamon
2 bananas, mashed
2 tablespoons dried cherries, finely chopped
1 recipe Cream Cheese Frosting, page 181

1. Preheat the oven to 350°F. Grease and flour two 8-inch cake pans.
2. In a mixing bowl, cream the canola oil and brown rice syrup at medium speed. Add the eggs one at a time, beating after each addition.
3. Sift the flour, carob powder, baking soda, and cinnamon onto a piece of waxed paper. Add the sifted ingredients to the egg-oil mixture and beat until combined. Fold in the mashed banana and dried cherries.
4. Divide the batter between the cake pans. Bake for 30 minutes or until a cake tester comes out clean. Allow the cake to cool in the pans for 10 minutes before removing the pans and transferring the cake to a cooling rack.
5. Allow the cake layers to cool completely before frosting. Frost with Cream Cheese Frosting.

Chapter 15

Flavor Enhancers

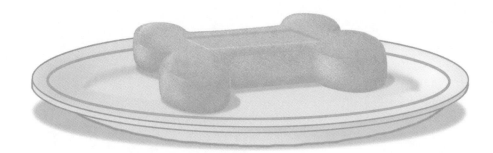

Barbecue Sauce

In this recipe, the sweet potato provides sweetness without adding sugar. Barbecue sauce always has a tomato base but can also include vinegar, assorted spices, brown sugar, molasses, pepper flakes, and even bourbon.

Yields 8 servings,
serving size ¼ cup

1 tablespoon virgin olive oil
2 cloves garlic, chopped
½ cup turkey sausage
2 tablespoons tomato paste
1 cup organic beef broth
½ cup sweet potato, cooked
    and mashed

57 Varieties

The first commercially produced barbecue sauce was introduced in 1948 by the H. J. Heinz Company. Heinz was founded in 1869 by Henry John Heinz, who began his business by delivering condiments to grocers via a horse-drawn wagon. The first products included horseradish, pickles, and tomato ketchup. Today, Heinz owns numerous brands, including Weight Watchers, Del Monte, and Boston Market.

1. In a heavy skillet, heat the olive oil and sauté the garlic until light brown. Remove the sausage casing and add the turkey meat to the pan, breaking it apart with a wooden spoon as it cooks. Continue cooking over medium-high heat for 7 minutes until sausage bits are brown and cooked through.

2. Add the tomato paste and cook for 1 minute. Add the beef broth, stirring to combine, and cook for 5 minutes.

3. Transfer the barbecue sauce to a blender or food processor. Add the cooked sweet potato and process until the sauce is smooth and creamy. If the sauce is too thick, add a bit more beef broth. Place ¼ cup barbecue sauce in your dog's bowl and serve mixed with kibble.

Chicken Gravy

If you don't have any cooked chicken available, you can boil raw chicken directly in the chicken broth. Served shredded with rice and water, this is a perfect meal for a dog with an upset stomach or diarrhea.

1. Place the frozen vegetables in a strainer and run them under hot water until defrosted.
2. Combine the vegetables, chicken broth, chicken, and rice in a blender or food processor. Process until the mixture is smooth and creamy. If it is too thick, add a bit more chicken broth. Place ¼ cup Chicken Gravy in your dog's bowl and heat in the microwave on high heat 20–25 seconds. Add kibble and stir until combined.

Yields 8 servings, serving size ¼ cup

½ cup frozen mixed peas and carrots
2 cups organic chicken broth
½ cup cooked chicken breast, shredded
½ cup rice, cooked

Turkey Gravy

As a special treat, serve your dog her own biscuits and gravy. Break up some savory flavored biscuits and spoon some warm turkey gravy over the top.

Yields 8 servings,
serving size ¼ cup

½ cup frozen mixed peas and
   carrots
2 cups organic beef broth
½ cup cooked turkey sausage
½ cup rice, cooked

1. Place the frozen vegetables in a strainer and run them under hot water until defrosted.
2. Combine the vegetables, beef broth, turkey sausage, and rice in a blender or food processor. Process until the mixture is smooth and creamy. If it is too thick, add a bit more beef broth. Place ¼ cup of the Turkey Gravy in your dog's bowl and heat in the microwave on high heat 20–25 seconds. Add kibble and stir until combined.

Biscuits and Gravy

A truck-stop favorite, biscuits and gravy are quintessentially American. The gravy is actually a white sauce made from the drippings of cooked pork sausage, white flour, and milk, laced with bits of sausage and served over warm country biscuits. The gravy is often highly seasoned with black pepper and is usually served for breakfast.

Mixed Vegetable Soup

Try using broccoli, green beans, spinach, and even apples in this recipe. The rice works as a thickening agent, adding creaminess at the same time. If you don't have any cooked rice available, you can always substitute cooked potato.

1. Place the frozen vegetables in a strainer and run them under hot water until defrosted.
2. Combine the vegetables, chicken broth, and rice in a blender or food processor. Process the mixture until it is smooth and creamy. If it is too thick, add a bit more chicken broth. Place ¼ cup of the soup in your dog's bowl and heat in the microwave on high heat 20–25 seconds. Add kibble and stir until combined.

Yield 8 servings, serving size ¼ cup

½ cup frozen mixed vegetables, or a combination of peas, carrots, and corn
1½ cups organic chicken broth
½ cup rice, cooked

Italian "Gravy"

Italian-Americans tend to refer to tomato sauce as "gravy." This phrase was coined when Italian immigrants tried to assimilate during the early 1900s. American brown gravy was never served at the table, but tomato sauce was and affectionately came to be known as "gravy."

Yields 8 servings, serving size ¼ cup

1 tablespoon virgin olive oil
2 cloves garlic, chopped
¼ cup carrot, finely chopped
1 cup crushed tomatoes
2 tablespoons Italian parsley, chopped
½ cup pasta, cooked
1 teaspoon Romano cheese, grated (optional)

1. Heat olive oil in a heavy saucepan and add the sliced garlic. Add the chopped carrots and cook over medium heat till caramelized.
2. Add the crushed tomatoes and continue cooking over medium heat for 10 minutes. Add the chopped parsley and stir to combine.
3. Place the cooked pasta in the food processor and pulse until it is slightly chopped. Add the pasta to the "gravy" and serve over kibble. Sprinkle with some freshly grated Romano cheese if desired.

Glorious Cheese

Pecorino Romano is a dry, granular, and sharp goat's milk cheese that is primarily used as a grating cheese. Parmigiano Reggiano, the classic Italian hard cheese made from raw cow's milk, has a nutty and fruity flavor that is eaten as a table cheese and with fruits and meats. It is also, of course, grated and served over meals. Each cheese has its own distinct flavor and aroma.

Salsa Verde

Italian salsa verde is usually served with boiled meats and consists of fresh herbs, garlic, capers, anchovies, lemon juice, and olive oil. Mexican salsa verde contains tomatillos, hot green chilies, garlic, and onion.

1. Place frozen spinach in a strainer and squeeze out the excess water.
2. Combine the spinach, chicken broth, parsley, anchovy, and rice in a blender or food processor. Process until the mixture is smooth and creamy. If it is too thick, add a bit more chicken broth. Place ¼ cup of the salsa in your dog's bowl and heat in the microwave on high heat 20–25 seconds. Add kibble and stir till combined.

Yields 8 servings, serving size ¼ cup

½ cup frozen chopped spinach, thawed
1½ cups organic chicken broth
2 tablespoons Italian parsley
1 unsalted anchovy fillet
½ cup rice, cooked

Salmon Gravy

Salmon is high in protein and is a great source of omega-3 fatty acids.

Yields 8 servings,
serving size ¼ cup

1½ cups organic chicken
    broth
½ cup canned salmon
½ cup frozen chopped
    broccoli, thawed
½ cup rice, cooked

Combine the chicken broth, salmon, broccoli, and rice in a blender or food processor. Process till the mixture is smooth and creamy. If it is too thick, add a bit more chicken broth. Place ¼ cup of the gravy in your dog's bowl and heat in the microwave on high heat 20–25 seconds. Add kibble and stir until combined.

Norse Mythology

Norse mythology relates the story of Loki, the god of mischief and strife. After killing Baldr, the god of beauty and light, Loki transformed himself into a salmon to escape the wrath of the other gods. They attempted to trap Loki in a net, but it was Thor who caught him by the tail with his hand. This explains why the salmon's tail is tapered.

Pea Soup

The soup will thicken in the refrigerator and will thin again as it is heated. During the summer, you can serve the soup cool thinned with a little extra chicken broth or water.

Combine the chicken broth, peas, cooked bacon, fresh mint, and rice in a blender, and process until smooth and creamy. If the mixture is too thick, add a bit more chicken broth. Place ¼ cup of the soup in your dog's bowl and heat in the microwave on high 20–25 seconds. Add kibble and stir until combined.

Yields 8 servings, serving size ¼ cup

2 cups organic chicken broth
1 cup frozen peas, thawed
1 piece Applegate Farms Sunday bacon, cooked
¼ cup fresh mint
½ cup rice, cooked

Mint

According to Greek mythology, Queen Persephone transformed a river nymph named Minthe into a sweet-smelling herb to avoid seduction by Hades, the god of the underworld. Mint grows prolifically near water, and the most common varieties are peppermint and spearmint. Both offer a cool, refreshing, aromatic flavor. Mint aids digestion and is a natural breath freshener.

Sloppy Joes

Try using ground turkey, chicken meat, or even turkey sausage if you don't want to offer your dog beef.

- -

Yields 8 servings,
serving size ¼ cup

4 ounces lean ground chuck
1 clove garlic, sliced
1½ cups organic beef broth
½ cup frozen peas, thawed
¼ cup prepared barbecue
  sauce
½ cup rice, cooked

1. Cook the ground chuck and garlic in a saucepan. Break apart with a fork and continue cooking until the meat is brown and no longer pink. Drain the cooked beef.
2. Combine the cooked ground beef, beef broth, peas, barbecue sauce, and rice in a blender or food processor. Process until the mixture is smooth and creamy. If it is too thick, add a bit more beef broth. Place ¼ cup of the sauce in your dog's bowl and heat in the microwave on high 20–25 seconds. Add kibble and stir until combined.

Sloppy Joe

Popularized in the 1950s, the sloppy joe actually referred to a type of pullover sweater. The style was worn oversized with the sleeves pushed up. A pair of unironed black pants completed the look, favored by teenage boys and girls. The term is still used today in parts of Australia and now simply refers to any type of pullover sweater.

Potato Soup

A bunch of fresh parsley would be a nice addition, as well as a piece of bacon. You can use a combination of different potatoes, but be sure to cut them roughly the same size so they cook at the same rate.

1. Heat the olive oil in a heavy stockpot over medium heat. Add the garlic and carrots and cook till they are caramelized, about 5 minutes.
2. Cut the potatoes into large chunks. There is no need to peel the potatoes unless you are using sweet potatoes. Add the potatoes and chicken broth to the pot and bring to a boil.
3. Lower the heat and cover the soup. Let simmer for 30 minutes or until the potatoes can easily be pierced with a fork. Cool slightly and pour the soup into a blender or food processor. Process until the soup is smooth and creamy. If it is too thick, add a bit more chicken broth. Place ¼ cup of the soup in your dog's bowl and heat in the microwave on high 20–25 seconds. Add kibble and stir until combined.

Yields 8 servings, serving size ¼ cup

1 tablespoon virgin olive oil
2 cloves garlic, chopped
½ carrot, finely chopped
4 potatoes, scrubbed
2 cups organic chicken broth

Cooking with Garlic

Fresh garlic is purchased as a bulb that is composed of many cloves. The easiest way to remove the skin is by placing the clove on a cutting board, laying the flat side of a chef's knife over it, and whacking the knife with the heel of your hand. The papery skin will peel off. You can also purchase peeled garlic, but it needs to be refrigerated and should be used within a month of purchase. Do not use garlic that has turned soft or has dried out.

Tomato, Anchovy, and Rice Soup

If you eliminate the rice and chicken broth, you can serve this savory tomato sauce with pasta for everyone in your family. Just skip the Parmesan cheese— adding cheese to a fish pasta sauce is an Italian culinary no-no.

Yields 8 servings,
serving size ¼ cup

1 tablespoon virgin olive oil
2 cloves garlic, chopped
2 unsalted anchovy fillets
1 cup crushed tomatoes
½ cup organic chicken broth
½ cup rice, cooked

1. Heat the olive oil in a heavy saucepan and add the sliced garlic. Add the anchovy fillets and use a wooden spoon to break them apart. The anchovies will melt and actually dissolve in the hot oil.
2. Add the crushed tomatoes and continue cooking over medium heat for 10 minutes.
3. Combine the cooked tomato sauce, chicken broth, and rice in a blender or food processor. Process until the soup is smooth and creamy. If the mixture is too thick, add a bit more chicken broth. Place ¼ cup of the soup in your dog's bowl. Add kibble and stir until combined.

Source Guide

Cooking Equipment and Supplies

Baking tools and ingredients
Pastry Chef Central
✍ *www.pastrychef.com*

Baking supplies, specialty
Fancy Flours
✍ *www.fancyflours.com*

Cookie cutters
Cookie Cutter Shop
✍ *www.cookiecuttershop.com*

Off the Beaten Path
Cookie cutters—excellent selection of dog- and cat-themed shapes
✍ *www.cookiecutter.com*

Ulu knives
Ulu.com
✍ *www.ulu.com*

Organic Foods

Basic Information

Healthy food guide and locator
Eat Well Guide
✍ *www.eatwellguide.org*

Organic Baking Ingredients

Flours, grains, mixes
King Arthur Flour
✍ *www.kingarthurflour.com*

Flours, grains, mixes, baking ingredients
✍ *www.worldpantry.com*

Whole-grain flours and gluten-free products
Bob's Red Mill
✍ *www.bobsredmill.com*

Organic Broths

Chicken, vegetable, and beef broths
Imagine
✍ *www.imaginefoods.com*

Organic Cheeses

Cheddar, Colby, Monterey Jack
Cedar Grove Cheese
✍ *www.cedargrovecheese.com*

Cheeses, eggs, and dairy products
Horizon Organic
✍ *www.horizonorganic.com*

Listing and links to Vermont cheese producers
Vermont Cheese Council
✍ *www.vtcheese.com*

Organic Meat Products

Beef, lamb, and pork
Niman Ranch
✍ *www.nimanranch.com*

Bison
BisonRidge Ranch
✍ *www.bisonridgeranch.com*

Organic Poultry Products

Chicken
Lobel's of New York
✍ *www.lobels.com*

Pet Health and Supplies

Dog Health Information

Advice on pet health, medication, pet care, and pet illnesses
PetEducation.com
✍ *www.peteducation.com*

Dog Products

Organic dog biscuits
robbie dawg, inc.
✍ *www.robbiedawg.com*

Dog toys made of organic cotton and dyes
Simply Fido
✍ *www.simplyfido.com*

Appendix B

Party Menus

Play Date

Peanut Butter, Carrot, and Wheat Germ Biscuits, page 34

Sweet Potato Pie Biscuits, page 40

Savory Bacon, Cheddar, and Oatmeal Biscuits, page 43

Sautéed Liver and Bacon Biscuits, page 50

Swiss Cheese on Rye Biscuits, page 52

Oatmeal, Date, and Cream Cheese Biscuits, page 58

Coconut Granola Bars, page 68

Outdoor Barbecue

Barbecued Chicken in a Biscuit, page 36

Bleu Cheese and Tomato Biscuits, page 54

BBQ Beef Biscotti, page 83

Kansas City BBQ Beef Tips, page 91

Chicken Pops, page 170

BBQ Buffalo Burgers, page 135

Banana Carob Chip Cake, page 182

Birthday Celebration

Green Apple and Turkey Sausage Biscuits, page 37

Pumpkin Pie Biscuits, page 39

Birthday Bacon Crumbles, page 62

Liver Paté Napoleons, page 63

Sardines and Potato Mash, page 151

Risotto and Spinach Cakes, page 159

Black Velvet Cake, page 191

Afternoon Tea Party

Peanut Butter Nibbles, page 90

Bleu Cheese Pop 'Ems, page 88

Ruby Hard-Boiled Eggs, page 109

Salmon Croquettes, page 147

Mini–Chicken Pot Pies, page 172

Pigs 'n Blankets, page 177

Rice Cake, page 186

Tuscan Retreat

Garlic Croutons, page 94

Pasta Crunchies, page 95

Sautéed Liver and Romano Cheese Biscuits, page 56

Roasted Tomato and Mozzarella Biscotti, page 77

Easy Chicken Parmigiana Tenders, page 124

Pasta with Olive Oil, Garlic, Zucchini, and Romano Cheese, page 155

Anchovy Baked Ziti, page 161

Index

We have Everything for Canine Care!

Trade Paperback, $14.95
ISBN 10: 1-58062-144-9
ISBN 13: 978-1-58062-144-1

Trade Paperback, $14.95
ISBN 10: 1-59337-320-1
ISBN 13: 978-1-59337-320-7

Trade Paperback, $14.95
ISBN 10: 1-59869-257-7
ISBN 13: 978-1-59869-257-0

Trade Paperback, $14.95
ISBN 10: 1-58062-666-1
ISBN 13: 978-1-58062-666-8

Trade Paperback, $14.95
ISBN 10: 1-58062-576-2
ISBN 13: 978-1-58062-576-0

Trade Paperback, $16.95
Semiconcealed Spiral Bound
ISBN 10: 1-59869-099-X
ISBN 13: 978-1-59869-099-6

Trade Paperback, $14.95
ISBN 10: 1-59337-419-4
ISBN 13: 978-1-59337-419-8